TRADITIONAL IRISH GUITAR

A tradition-based approach to
accompaniment and solo-playing
of Irish dance music on the guitar

Paul de Grae

OSSIAN

Acknowledgements

I'm glad of the opportunity to thank some fine musicians with whom I've spent many happy hours, and from whom I hope I've learned a lot - in particular my wife Deirdre Sullivan, Kathleen Mulcahy, Ciarán Dalton, Kevin Ryan, Rory Costello, the late Tom McCarthy, and the late Ned Nolan, who were my "local team" when I came to Kerry.

Also Máire O'Keeffe, Jackie Daly, Aoife O'Keeffe, Pádraig Ó Broin, Gerry Harrington, Eoghan O'Sullivan, Steve Cooney, Mick, Jim and Jack Culloty, Patsy Broderick, Michelle O'Sullivan, Tom Traynor, Donal Murphy, John Larkin, Eoin Duignan, Joe Thoma, Maurice McKenna, and many others.

I also want to thank former Kerry County Arts Officer Clare Brownen for good advice and encouragement, Catherine Considine for making the recording such a fun job to do, and The Traditional Music Archive for information on tune titles, etc. I'm grateful to Joe Thoma and Paul S. Cranford for permission to include their original compositions.

Published by
Ossian Publications
14-15 Berners Street, London W1T 3LJ, UK.

Exclusive Distributors:
Music Sales Limited
Distribution Centre, Newmarket Road,
Bury St Edmunds, Suffolk IP33 3YB, UK.
Music Sales Corporation
257 Park Avenue South, New York, NY10010
United States Of America.
Music Sales Pty Limited
120 Rothschild Avenue,
Rosebery, NSW 2018, Australia.

Order No. OMB220
ISBN 13: 978-1-84609-626-6
© Paul de Grae 1989
This book © Copyright 1996 Novello & Company Limited,
part of The Music Sales Group.

Photography & layout by John Loesberg.

Printed in the EU.

www.musicsales.com

CONTENTS

This book is dedicated to my parents Tom and Nora Gray.

INTRODUCTION

Because the guitar is not regarded as a traditional instrument in Ireland, there is no generally accepted system of teaching traditional Irish music on the guitar, and no definable style to learn. As a result, and despite the example of some outstanding guitarists, the guitar has yet to be fully absorbed into Irish music.

The idea of the guitar as a foreign instrument loses some of its force when you consider that, of the traditional instruments used in Ireland today, only the whistle, pipes and harp can claim a native origin (fiddles, or *fidle*, were played in medieval Ireland, but whatever these were, they were not the same as the modern violin, which was developed in 16th century Italy).

The guitar is older than that archetypal Irish instrument, the uileann pipes, and much older than the accordion and concertina. It is the most important traditional instrument in Spanish music, and its ancestor the *'ud* (in Arabic, *al 'ud*, hence the English word *lute*) is still widespread in the traditional and classical music of the Middle East.

Until recently the guitar was a rarity in Irish traditional music, but this is because of social and historical rather than musical reasons. By the time the guitar arrived on the scene in Ireland, the native musical tradition - which might have absorbed it and evolved a traditional style of playing, as with the accordion - was in decline. A culture in decline tends to be conservative, and the guitar smelled suspiciously of youth and brash modernism, not to mention being the icon of the rock & roll culture. Despite its popularity in the 'ballad boom' of the 1960s (or who knows, because of that as well) the gap between guitarists and traditional musicians remained wide.

The purpose of this book is to bridge that gap: to help a moderately competent guitar player - you, I hope - to become proficient in traditional Irish music both as a soloist and as an accompanist, and to be able to join in with traditional musicians as an equal partner.

Guitarists who try their hands at traditional music have usually already learned to play in some other style - rock, jazz, fingerstyle, classical or plain old three-chord strumming - and tend to adapt the music to the guitar style, rather than vice versa. Instead, this book presents a style of playing which is based in the tradition but not bound by it, and aims to explain some things about Irish music and how it has been played and accompanied in the past.

PART 1 takes a brief look at the nature of traditional Irish music, and at the development of accompaniment in the early recordings, the ceili bands, and present-day traditional-based performers.

With the new style goes a new tuning, or rather an existing tuning put to new use; this is described in **PART 2**. Although most of the music in the book has been arranged with this tuning in mind, it can also be played in standard tuning or DADGAD if you prefer.

PART 3: ACCOMPANIED TUNES and **PART 4: SOLO TUNES** form the heart of the book. There are 25 tunes in each section, a mixture of jigs, reels, and hornpipes, plus a few polkas, slides and highlands. Some are appearing in print for the first time, and others are well-known, although the settings here include variations and arrangements not found elsewhere. The text covers points of style and technique, and there are sections on chord substitution, rhythm, ornamentation and variation.

In the case of accompanied tunes, the tune, and sometimes the accompaniment, is written in staff notation, with chords underneath. Some accompaniments are also presented in tablature form, and the solo tunes are all given in both staff notation and tablature form. Tablature is mostly for the tuning described in Part 2.

No strict division is intended between solo and accompanied tunes. Chords are given for backing most of the solo tunes, and similarly the accompanied tunes could well be played as solos.

Most of the tunes in this book have been taken, directly or indirectly, from the playing of traditional musicians in Ireland, while the exception (*Elvis Presley's Jig*) is not meant to be taken too seriously.

There are no slow airs in this collection, but not because they don't suit the guitar. Slow airs can be adapted very successfully to the guitar, with the addition of a few bass notes and a careful attention to phrasing and ornament (slide guitar can be very effective). However, it's almost impossible to show on paper the subtleties of timing and phrasing which are essential to the playing of slow airs. It's very personal music, and the best way to learn airs is by listening to a good singer or instrumentalist. Having some idea of the words is a help. You can use books such as 'Ceolta Gael' by Seán Óg and Mánus Ó Baoill, or O'Neill's 'Music of Ireland' and 'Waifs and Strays of Gaelic Melody', but rely on your ear first. You can also try playing some dance tunes as slow airs (on the recording, *The Humours of Tullycrine* is played first as a slow air, and then in the hornpipe arrangement given on page 34).

The book concludes with **PART 5: BOOKS** and **PART 6: RECORDINGS**. These are personal selections rather than definitive listings. Part 5 includes a list of other printed settings of the tunes in this book.

MUSIC NOTATION

You don't have to read music in order to play it, but it helps. Fortunately, traditional Irish music is fairly easy to read, since each tune has just a single line of melody.

Tablature is useful if you don't read music, or if you're using an unfamiliar tuning such as the one described in Part 2. The lines represent the six strings of the guitar (1st string at the top) and the numbers refer to the frets, '0' being an open string. The relative length of the notes is shown in the same way as on staff notation. For the tunes in this book all you need to remember is:

1. Notes linked by a single line (or with a single hook on the stem) are each half as long as notes which are not linked together.

2. Notes linked by a double line are each half as long as notes linked by a single line, and a quarter as long as notes which are not linked together.

3. A dot after a note increases its time value by half.

4. A triplet, in reels and hornpipes, consists of three notes played in the time of two, and is indicated like this:

5. A double bar line with dots on one side or on both sides means that the part of the tune on the side of the dots should be repeated.

A point to note in connection with both tablature and standard music notation is that traditional tunes are *written* as if the notes were generally of equal length, but are *played* differently. The first note of a group of quavers should usually be slightly longer, and in the case of reels and especially hornpipes, where the quavers typically come in groups of four, the third note is also lengthened, although not as much as the first. The idea is similar to the *notes inégales* of 18th-century French harpsichord music (so there).

Jig:	written as	♪♪♪	played as	♪.♪♪
Reel or hornpipe:	written as	♪♪♪♪	played as	♪.♪♪.♪

HOW FAST ?

There's no law about the speed at which these tunes should be played. Fashion, personal taste, local custom, the mood of the moment, and the needs of dancers may each have an influence. Still, a rough guide may be better than nothing. The following metronome settings are recommended by Breandán Breathnach in 'Ceol Rince na hÉireann':

reels:	♩ = 224
double jigs:	♩. = 127
slip jigs:	♩. = 144
hornpipes:	♩ = 180
polkas:	♩ = 137

ABOUT THE RECORDING

The recording has 15 tracks, containing 31 of the tunes in this book, grouped into sets. Tunes marked with an asterisk (*) in the text are on the recording. Most of the tunes are played on double-tracked acoustic guitar, and at a moderate speed so that you can play along. To vary the sound, in some cases a capo is used, and on some tracks the melody is played on electric guitar. See the liner notes for details of capo positions, tuning, etc.

The variation and ornamentation of traditional tunes is examined at some length later in the book. In connection with the recording, it's enough to mention that the tunes as played inevitably differ in minor details from the printed settings.

PART 1: TRADITIONAL IRISH MUSIC AND ITS ACCOMPANIMENT

Anyone who has tried to sing chart hits unaccompanied at a party or in the shower will know that, unlike traditional tunes, such music doesn't really work without the backing. By contrast, in Irish traditional music, as in most folk music, the notes come one at a time as a single stream of melody, without the harmony or chords you find in classical or popular music. In technical terms, it is *melodic* rather than *harmonic* in character.

The most basic instrument of all is the unaccompanied human voice, so it's easy to see why folk music leans more towards melody than harmony, and the purest form of traditional music is still the solo singer or musician.

The traditional instruments closest in expressive power to the human voice are the fiddle, flute, whistle and pipes. Chords can't be played on the flute or whistle, and while possible on the fiddle, they are rarely used in Irish music. The uileann pipes are a special case, since they have a system of drones and a limited range of chords on the regulators; but these are used mainly for occasional special effects, as much rhythmic as harmonic, and it is reasonable to class the pipes also as melodic rather than harmonic.

Other established traditional instruments are the metal-reed family, including the melodeon, button-accordion, piano-accordion, concertina and (less commonly) the harmonica. Harmonies are possible on all these instruments, especially the accordions. As with the pipes, however, these tend to be used more for rhythmic emphasis than for accompaniment, although there are some outstanding players of both instruments who make good use of the harmonic possibilities.

AN APPROACH TO ACCOMPANIMENT

In its origins, traditional Irish music is essentially a solo art. Even today if you wander into an informal session and find, let's say, two fiddles, a flute and an accordion playing *The Silver Spear*, what you will hear is the sound of four solo versions played simultaneously. Whether or not the result is a treat to listen to will partly depend on how different these versions are from each other (the musical ability of the players will also have something to do with it, of course).

Some of the differences you will hear arise from the nature of the different instruments. Other factors include the personality of the individual musician, the local playing style, the influence of recorded or printed versions, and so on.

Sometimes one musician may play an octave below the others, if the tune is suitable. This is common in Donegal music, and from the other end of the country examples can be heard on recordings of Kerry fiddlers Pádraig O'Keeffe, Denis Murphy and Julia Clifford. But most of the time, when two or more traditional musicians are playing together they play the melody in unison.

Although Irish melodies in their traditional form are unharmonised, they do fit into a scale or key, whether it be the major or minor scales of conventional musicology or one of the more wayward modes beloved of folk musicians everywhere. Usually the tune itself will give a hint as to what chords to use. For example, here is the opening of the well-known hornpipe *The Harvest Home*:

The first bar contains the notes of the chord of D major, the third bar suggests and then confirms a change to A7, and so on. These are fairly obvious chord changes. Now let's look at a more difficult tune, the reel *Rakish Paddy*.

This seems to start in C, or perhaps A minor, but instead of following the 'three-chord-trick' of the key of C (chords of C, F and G), it moves into D major, and eventually finishes there. Don't be misled by the key signature: it is usual in writing out traditional music to indicate only those sharps or flats which actually recur in the melody - it saves having to write a lot of accidentals - so a key signature of one sharp does not necessarily mean the key of G.

Anyhow, this is only the first part of a two-part tune; the second part is even more unpredictable.

The melody suggests various chords, but none very definitely; should it be G, C or perhaps E minor in the first bar?

The thing about *Rakish Paddy*, as with many of the more interesting tunes in the Irish tradition, is that the melody is just too wayward to be tied down to a chord sequence. One solution is to take a leaf from the pipers' book and play the melody on the higher strings of the guitar, adding reinforcement on the bass strings ('drones') or in the form of partial chords ('regulators'). In accompaniment, use chords that are open enough to allow the melody to go where it likes without clashing with the chords.

Accompaniment, in the usual sense of playing chords or counter-melodies along with the tune, is a relatively modern grafting on to the root-stock of traditional Irish music, and reflects a gradual change in attitudes among both musicians and listeners. Two key factors were the early recordings and the ceili bands. Each of these topics deserves a book to itself, but a brief summary may help to illustrate the development of accompaniment in Irish music.

THE EARLY RECORDINGS

Traditional Irish music on records began in America.   The phonograph industry there in the early years of this century soon realised that, with the large numbers of immigrants living in America, there was a ready market for ethnic recordings of all types.   Not only Irish, but Italian, Yiddish, Balkans, Eastern European, Latin American, and of course African-American blues musicians were recorded, and the records sold in large numbers. Music hall artists incorporated elements of various ethnic cultures in their acts, and many weird and wonderful 'Irish melodies' were unleashed on the public.

An example of the happy disregard for cultural boundaries at that time is the career of the German-American melodeon player John J. Kimmel, whose superb playing of Irish music earned him the popular nickname 'The Irish Dutchman'.

Ethnic and commercial music had an influence on each other, and in Irish music, accompaniment on piano, guitar or small band gradually crossed over from the popular music of the day. A comparison of recordings by, for example, the pipers Patsy Tuohey in the early 1920s and Tom Ennis in the late 1920s and early 1930s shows the changing approach to the presentation of the music. Tuohey's only accompaniment was his regulators (keys set into the stock of the pipes and providing a limited system of chords), while Ennis recorded with piano backing. Piano was also used on recordings of such fiddlers as James Morrison, Michael Coleman, and Paddy Killoran, and melodeon player John J. Kimmel.

By the 1930s some of these players used guitar accompaniment (Coleman's recording of *Lord Gordon's Reel* has what sounds like a tenor guitar on it), but as with most of the piano accompaniment, the guitar playing tended to be pretty basic and did not add much to the performance. An honourable exception to the general low standard of guitar accompanists was Martin Christi, whose jazzy backing enlivened several of James Morrison's recordings (*The Blackberry Blossom* is one example); Morrison seems to have been more fortunate, or perhaps more selective, than others in his choice of band members.

Just a few years later, an interesting style of accompaniment was developed in the Shetlands by the guitarist Willie Johnson. Through 78s and short-wave radio, Willie was familiar with the music of the great American jazz guitarists such as Eddie Lang, Eddie Durham and Lonnie Johnson, and he began to adapt their swing-band style to the accompaniment of Shetland fiddle music, as Martin Christi appears to have done for Irish music. In the Shetlands, accompaniment is much more a part of the traditional music than in Ireland, so in a sense there was already a place set for the guitar. Willie's combination of American swing and Shetland tradition was a very successful blend, and the 'Shetland swing' style, as it's called, is now an integral part of the traditional music there. It is characterised by a driving rhythm, damped chords, and the use of jazz elements such as syncopation and passing chords. Happily, Willie is still very much with us, and can be heard on recordings by Shetland fiddlers Aly Bain and Tom Anderson (often with pianist Violet Tulloch also).

CEILI BANDS AND RECENT TRENDS

The rise of the ceili bands partly overlaps the development of the early recordings. As American 78s became available in Ireland their influence spread rapidly, and the change to a more professional and generally fuller-sounding music was accelerated by a radical change in the context in which the dance music was played.

The greater mobility brought about by modern transport combined with the spread of commercial dance halls to bring about a rapid decline in the house dances and crossroads dances which had been the main musical entertainments in the peasant culture of the 18th and 19th centuries - the period from which most of our stock of traditional music dates. The change in the musical environment in the early part of this century was not one of the happier chapters in Irish social history. The story of that era, including the unedifying campaign which led to the passing of the 1936 Public Dance-Halls Act, is best told in Breandán Breathnach's excellent booklet 'Dancing in Ireland' (Dal gCais Publications, 1983).

The effect was to take the music out of the comparatively intimate and domestic setting of the old Irish social dances, and put it in the more formal context of the dance hall. The musicians were eased out of their fireside seats, dressed in Sunday clothes, and put up on a stage with microphones. The ceili band was born.

Playing long hours in often crowded and noisy halls, the musicians of the ceili bands needed the unifying force provided by a solid accompaniment, whether performed on piano alone or, in the larger bands, by a full rhythm section of piano, guitar or banjo, bass and drums. Typically the melody would be played on a combination of accordion, fiddle, flute, whistle and banjo, often with the addition of such imports from the popular music field as the saxophone or clarinet.

Songs and tunes were borrowed in the same way, the repertoire being tailored to suit the occasion; and despite the mixed pedigree, many of these bands were (and are) very good indeed. Whether they should be described as Irish dance bands influenced by popular music, or vice versa, is a conundrum I happily leave to the experts.

The relevant point is that here, as with the Irish-American recordings and the Shetland swing style, is an historical precedent for the combination of traditional music and modern influences - a trend that has accelerated since the 1960s as the music has been taken up by players from outside what might be called the true traditional base.

In the late 1960s and 1970s, the development of an indigenous modern approach to Irish music by Sweeney's Men, Planxty, The Bothy Band, De Danann, Paul Brady, Clannad and others, captured the interest of a new generation who had been listening to Bob Dylan or The Rolling Stones before they ever heard of Pádraig O'Keeffe or Willie Clancy, and who previously would not have known a hornpipe from a gaspipe. The members of these pioneering groups - and I don't mean to portray them as ancient monuments, since they are still making good music - all had a firm grounding in real traditional music, but their treatment of it reflects an awareness of the other musical styles known to their audience, as well as a more professional approach to performance. All this has encouraged an interest in the music among people (like me) with no background in 'the tradition', and has helped to ensure its survival in one form or another for at least another generation.

CONCLUSIONS

Admittedly this blending of styles has produced some regrettable drivel over the years, but the myth that that there is only one way to play Irish music can no longer be sustained. As with all music worthy of the name, it must be played with respect and understanding, but I don't believe that a modern musician needs to be bound strictly by the stylistic conventions of the culture in which that music originated.

Such conventions are useful academic descriptions rather than articles of faith, and in any case they have been cheerfully ignored by folk musicians themselves, who thought nothing of including in their repertoire waltzes, polkas, schottisches, tunes from travelling shows, parlour ballads and Carolan airs alongside the 'pure-bred' jigs, reels and hornpipes - much to the scholarly disdain of some early folk music collectors, who deplored what they saw as the degeneration of the native music.

The most reliable basis for the appreciation of Irish music is to study its history, listen to recordings of all types from the rough-but-authentic to the modern professional, and try if you can to hear the music in its most natural and enjoyable setting in the houses and pubs of Ireland. After that, just play it as it sounds right to you.

PART 2: TUNINGS & CHORDS

Standard guitar tuning (EADGBE, 6th string to 1st) is a wonderfully versatile tuning - what else did Segovia and Chuck Berry have in common? - but it can have disadvantages in playing Irish music, whether solo or in accompaniment. Chords in standard tuning provide close harmonies that may not suit the melody, which is often a free-range creature, not easily harnessed to a rigid chord structure. In solo playing, there is not much chance to let open strings sound on after striking, which would give resonance to the overall sound. An Irish tune played solo on guitar in standard tuning can sound rather thin (unless of course you have the technique of an Arty McGlynn to bring it to life - in which case you don't need this book).

There is an important difference between tunes played on a guitar in standard tuning and tunes played on instruments such as the banjo, mandolin, and bouzouki. This involves the principle of *sympathetic vibration*, whereby a string that is not actually played will vibrate in sympathy with the string that *is* played, when the note to which it is tuned is sounded. For example, if you play a D on the second string of the guitar, it will cause the open 4th string (tuned to D an octave lower) to sound. This works not only with octaves, but to a lesser extent also with fifths (doh/soh); in theory it works for every note in the chromatic scale, but the other notes respond at an increasingly higher pitch and much more faintly.

The Indian sitar and the Hardanger fiddle of Scandinavia both make use of sympathetic vibration, with varying numbers of sympathetic strings passing under the main strings.

The tuning of a mandolin (GDAE, the same as a fiddle) or a tenor banjo (the same an octave lower) is such that the sympathetic vibration of open strings usually fits with the tune being played, the bulk of Irish melodies being in the keys of G, D and A major, and A and E minor (bouzouki tuning varies, but one common tuning is GDAD). On guitar in standard tuning, the sympathetic vibration of open strings is often not sympathetic at all, in the ordinary sense.

Like many guitar players, I began some years ago to experiment with non-standard tunings. The first and most obvious was simply to tune the 6th string down to D; this is called *drop-D* tuning. It gives a satisfying depth in the bass range, and is fine as far as it goes, although the comments above about Irish tunes played in standard tuning still apply.

The open tunings of G (DGDGBD), C (CGCGCE) and D (DADF#AD) are useful for other types of music, but are a bit too definite in tonality for Irish music, besides restricting the freedom to play in other keys.

The *modal-D* tuning (DADGAD) invented by Davy Graham is probably the most common non-standard tuning for flat-pickers playing Irish music, whether solo or accompaniment. In fingerstyle, it's widely used in so-called Celtic music, excellently by Bert Jansch, John Renbourn and Pierre Bensusan, for example. This tuning is examined in Sarah McQuaid's 'The

Irish DADGAD Guitar Book and Tape' (Ossian). Unless you're fairly nifty or use a capo, however, it can restrict your choice of key, or so I find anyhow - all those nice ringing open strings inevitably suggest the key of D.

A variation on DADGAD is *low-C* tuning (CGDGAD), which is full of interesting possibilities for fingerstyle playing of traditional tunes, but which I have found to be less useful for flat-picking and accompaniment.

I wanted a tuning that could be used in all the common keys in Irish music, preferably without the need for a capo - I have yet to find a capo that doesn't put the guitar at least slightly out of tune - and which would avoid the close harmonies of standard tuning without going too far into the 'drone zone' of some of the alternative tunings. The tuning which I eventually found most satisfactory is one invented by the great English singer and guitarist, Martin Carthy: **DADEAE**.

The intervals between the strings are similar to DADGAD moved down a string (more so in the variant tuning occasionally used by Martin Carthy, EADEAE). Using DADEAE, you can easily play in D major or minor, A major or minor, E minor and to a lesser extent G major. The use of a capo at the fifth fret permits easier playing in the key of G, using D shapes, and an alternative way of playing in D, using A shapes.

A useful effect for backing Irish tunes is that you can hedge your bets about the chords you play: instead of the very specific chords in standard tuning, you can use chords with open string drones, which fill out the melody while omitting some of the notes which might clash with it - handy if you're not too sure what chord you should be playing anyway.

The strings to change from standard tuning are the 2nd, 3rd and 6th. The 3rd string is tuned one and a half tones below standard, and if the action on your guitar is low you may need to use a slightly heavier gauge string. I use standard light gauge strings (.012 to .053 or thereabouts), and they don't seem to floppy. As with other tunings, beware of breaking strings if you frequently change back and forth from standard.

I'd call DADEAE 'Carthy tuning' except that Martin has since modified it for his own use, first to DADEAB and later all down a tone to CGCDGA. I haven't followed him in this, because I found DADEAE such a useful tuning for Irish music, so I'll call it 'Irish tuning' from here on - even though it was invented by an Englishman.

'Irish tuning' does take some getting used to, but I have found it to be the most rewarding for Irish music, and it's worth giving it at least one try; the tablature should help. If you prefer to use standard, drop-D or DADGAD, you can still play the music in this book anyway, and tablature is given for some tunes in drop-D tuning. But it really doesn't matter what tuning you prefer - play in open B flat 9th diminished if it works for you.

CHORDS

The appeal of Irish tuning is that it offers an escape from the strait-jacket of chord sequences, but a knowledge of some basic chords is essential. The following diagrams show the most useful chords in various positions. The numbers at the left of the diagrams refer to the frets. "O" means an open string, and 'X' means a string which should not be played; where an 'X' string occurs in the middle of a chord, it should be muted with the pad of the nearest finger.

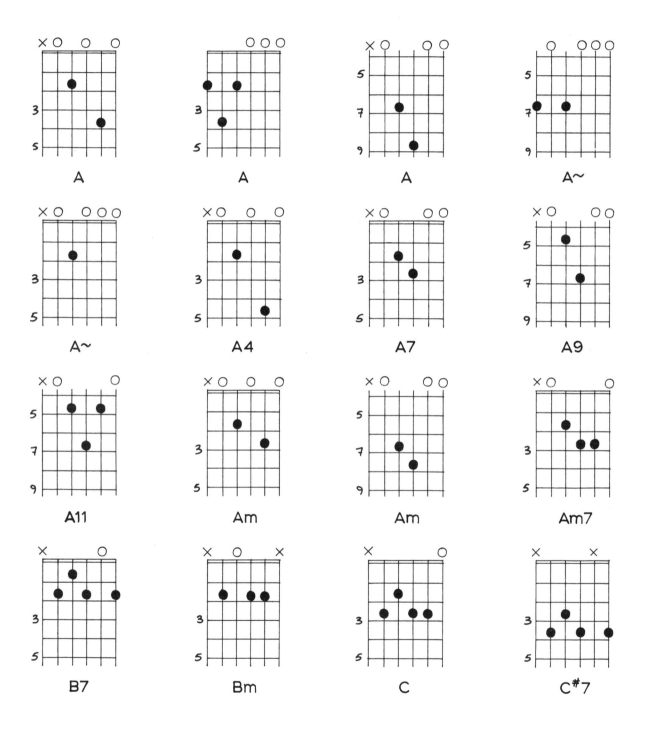

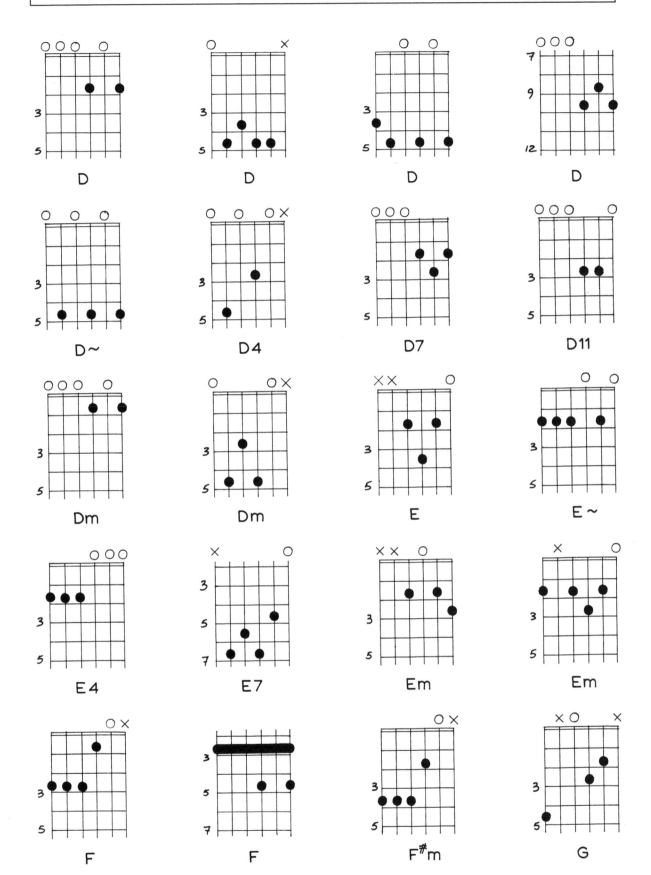

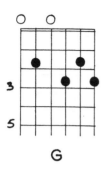

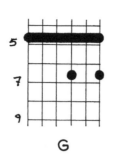

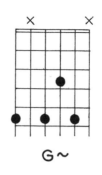

G   G   G~   G~

The chords marked with a squiggle (A~, etc.) are neither major nor minor, being composed of octaves (low and high doh) and fifths (doh/soh), omitting the third note of the scale (mi). This is a note which may clash with the melody as it weaves its way up and down the scale, whereas fifths seem to absorb dissonance more easily.

A useful effect is to play open-string drones against a contrasting chord or partial chord. For example, instead of changing from A minor to G major and back (a common alternation in A minor tunes) you can play elements of a G chord against a background of A and E drone strings:

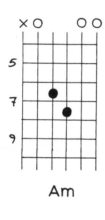

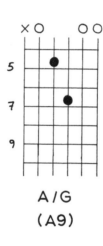

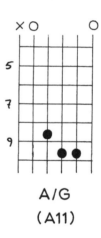

Am   A / G   A / G
                    (A9)   (A11)

This is less abrupt than changing to the full chord of G, and lets the music flow more freely - although of course it will be better to change to G in some cases. The accompaniment to *Old John's Jig* (pages 29 & 33) uses this technique.

Similarly in A major, a range of partial chords is available on the inner strings; these are used on the accompaniment to *Up the Track* (page 52). The A/E chord is simply moved down two frets to become the A/D chord:

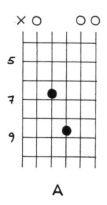

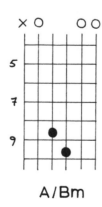

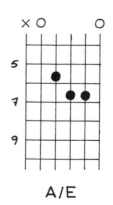

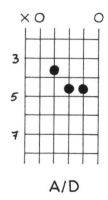

A   A / Bm   A / E   A / D

18

With a little experimenting, you'll find that this technique can be used for other chord combinations - D/C, D/G, Em/D, and so on.

In *drop-D* tuning, all D-based chords can have an open 6th string. Any chords which in standard tuning have an open 6th string must be modified by either omitting the 6th string or fretting it at the second fret; and the fingering of some other chords is slightly changed. Examples are shown below.

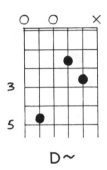

D~

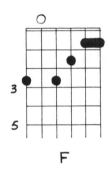

F

G

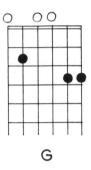

G

Finally, some slightly unusual chords in standard tuning which are used for some tunes in this book; these are also suitable for drop-D, adding, omitting or fretting the 6th string where necessary.

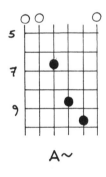

A~

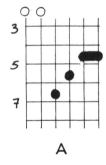

A

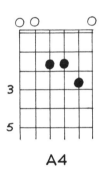

A4

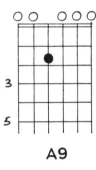

A9

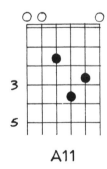

A11

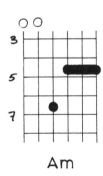

Am

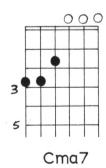

Cma7

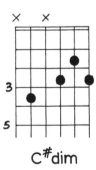

C#dim

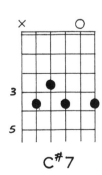

C#7

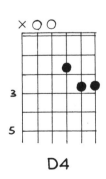

D4

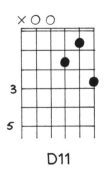

D11

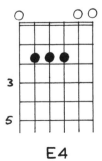

E4

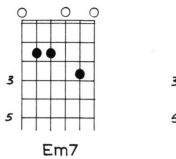

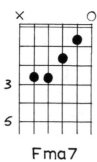

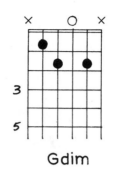

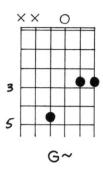

Em7   Fma7   Gdim   G~

Chord substitution - replacing the obvious chord with an interesting alternative - is discussed on page 30.

A DIGRESSION ON TUNING

This bit is for people who share my obsession with tuning - the rest of you, feel free to skip it. But if you run into problems tuning your guitar in DADGAD or in Irish tuning, read on...

The theory of tuning is far too complicated to be covered in detail here, but it may be helpful to mention that there is no such thing as universally correct pitch. All tuning systems involve some sort of compromise in the pitch of the notes of the scale (consult a good music dictionary or encyclopædia if you're interested in the mathematical explanation of this).

In the *equal temperament* system generally used today, all semitones are equal, which oddly enough means that all intervals except the octave are slightly out of tune compared to the natural scale (see below). But it also means that a note is the same no matter what key it's in - the same note A is *doh* in the key of A, *soh* in the key of D, *re* in the key of G, and so on. The advantage of this is that a fixed-note instrument such as a piano or any fretted instrument can be played in tune in any key. Imagine if you had to move the frets of the guitar to suit the key you wanted to play in (Indian music does not use equal temperament, and the sitar has adjustable frets for just this reason).

Violins and other non-fretted string instruments can be played in either equal temperament or the older *natural scale*, which to most of us nowadays sounds out of tune, more so at some notes of the scale than others. The natural scale is what you get if you tune using harmonics, and is based on principles discovered by Pythagoras in the 6th century BC (again, check your encyclopædia). It's fine for traditional singing and for instruments of adjustable pitch, if there is little or no harmony and the range of keys is not great, but it fell out of favour in the late 18th century as classical music became more adventurous.

It seems to me that some traditional musicians are more inclined to play in the natural scale - particularly some older players, who perhaps are closer to the music in its original form. Sometimes, a musician is simply out of tune by any definition, or may alter some notes for expressive purposes; but if the fifths (*soh* notes) seem consistently sharp and the thirds (*mi* notes) consistently flat, he or she may be using the natural scale.

On stringed instruments tuned entirely or partly in fifths (fiddle, mandolin, banjo, and guitar in DADGAD or in Irish tuning) there is a tendency to tune to something like the natural scale, because of the resonance of the fifths. This can be a problem on the guitar, particularly if you tune to seventh fret harmonics. The twelfth fret gives you an octave harmonic, which is fine, but the seventh fret harmonic gives you a 'natural' 5th. In equal temperament the 5th is slightly flattened, and your frets are marked out in accordance with this system. So if you tune a second string A to the seventh fret harmonic on the fourth string, you'll find that the D on the fifth fret of the second string is slightly sharp compared with the D on the open fourth string. It may be consoling to know that this is not the fault of your guitar or your ear.

Short of getting a fretless guitar, there's not a lot you can do about this - you can't be in tune with both the natural 5ths and the frets, and with sympathetic vibration you'll be quite conscious of the open strings. In my opinion, tuning to the frets is better than tuning to harmonics, but go with what suits you best.

Kate Mulcahy

PART 3: ACCOMPANIED TUNES.

There are 25 tunes in this section, some with full written accompaniment and some with chords only. Use the music along with the recording, where applicable. Playing along with your favourite albums is good practice too, for both solo playing and accompaniment. By altering the speaker balance, you may be able to turn down the original accompaniment, if any, and do your own thing: be De Danann's rhythm guitarist in the privacy of your own home!

SESSION ETIQUETTE

Before getting down to the music, it may be useful to say something about playing at informal sessions, in a pub, at a fleadh, or wherever.

The guitar has not always blended happily with Irish music, and some traditional musicians have a healthy suspicion of the instrument - perhaps based on the experience of having a good session ruined by an over-enthusiastic three-chord-basher, perhaps an instinctive aversion to the rock & roll connotations of guitars in general. And some musicians just sound better without accompaniment. So try not to take it personally if some people start muttering darkly when they see you come in with your guitar.

Fortunately this sort of thing doesn't happen that often, and in recent years, as standards have improved, guitarists have become much more accepted as part of the traditional scene. Many traditional players (not only the younger ones) actively seek out accompaniment nowadays, and while this is not altogether a welcome development, it does make guitarists feel more accepted. If you can play well, or even just adequately, and show respect and understanding for the music, you'll soon fit in. Traditional musicians are friendly creatures in general, and they know that more traditional hazards such as too many bodhráns or a bad accordion are much more disruptive than a bit of tasteful guitar picking.

Of course, it's only good manners to ask people if they mind you joining in; that goes for any musician, not just guitarists (see Ciarán Carson's 'Pocket Guide to Irish Traditional Music' for an entertaining discourse on session etiquette in general, including the perennially important subject of buying drink for the musicians).

An important point to remember is: don't try to play along with a tune if you don't know it - not unless you have developed a thorough understanding of traditional Irish music and are good at musical guessing games. This may seem like stating the obvious, but it's amazing how many people assume that traditional music must be simple music (created by peasants for peasants, etc.) and that any competent musician should be able to accompany it on first hearing. Well, it ain't necessarily so, and in fact orthodox classical training may even be a hindrance since, as mentioned earlier, traditional music is often in modes which are unfamiliar to the classically-trained ear.

Having said that, many tunes are straightforward enough from the accompanist's point of view. If a tune is new to you, let the other musicians play it through once and then join in on the repeat if you think you've got the hang of it. If this happens in the middle of a set of tunes, you can either stop playing altogether or doodle away on a drone string until you find your bearings.

RHYTHM

Irish traditional music is played in only a few simple time signatures - mainly 4/4 (reels and hornpipes) and 6/8 (jigs), and to a much lesser extent 9/8 (slip jigs), 12/8 (slides and some single jigs) and 2/4 (polkas and single reels). So there is no great difficulty for an accompanist in providing a basic beat, and this gives you a chance to work on some of the more subtle aspects of phrasing, syncopation, and so on.

In the nature of things, accompaniment is not an end in itself - it's there to support the melody. In Irish music, where melody and accompaniment are played on separate instruments, the accompaniment must be tailored to suit the melody player or players. This requires a certain amount of versatility, since a style that suits one player may not suit another. I can't over-emphasise the importance of listening to a player's style before attempting to accompany him or her. Within the apparently simple bounds of 4/4 or 6/8, there may be many nuances of phrasing which a careless accompaniment may obscure.

Broadly speaking, there are two main types of accompaniment in Irish music (apart from good and bad, that is). In the older, ceili band style, the accompaniment is straight-ahead, directly on the beat, and with little in the way of fancy business. This is a great all-purpose style, and played well, it can be as exciting as old-fashioned rock & roll. If played too rigidly, it can become boring, but at least it is unlikely to upset the melody player's timing - accenting the beat in this regular way is a wonderful support to a player.

A more modern style was pioneered on guitar by Paul Brady, using strumming techniques more associated with rock music. This approach allows the accompanist to accent the tune in a way that responds to the phrasing, rather than following a strict 4/4 or whatever. Syncopation (off-beat accenting) of the melody itself is common enough in the Irish idiom, and this can be reinforced very effectively in the accompaniment. On the other hand, some older players may find this sort of backing too 'jazzy', and indeed it doesn't suit every tune.

There are no hard and fast rules about any of this, and I've mostly avoided specifying a rhythmic style for the tunes in this book. It's up to you to make your own assessment of how to go about it, based on your knowledge of the tune and the players. As always, keep your ears open to what the others are up to, and try to respond to their phrasing.

Now to the music, beginning with some fairly simple tunes that need just a few easy chords. As mentioned before, many of the finest Irish tunes are by nature too wayward to be tied down to a chord sequence, but equally there are many tunes of charm and interest which work well with a simple backing.

In some tunes, including the first two, the melody line is shown on the upper stave, with the accompaniment on the stave below and separately in tablature form. The diagonal lines on the lower stave and on the tablature represent the chords, the name of the chord (D, A, etc.) being written above the accompaniment stave.

For most other tunes, chords are shown under the melody line. Chords in brackets are optional. Refer to Part 2 for any unfamiliar chords.

In the melody, remember the *notes inégales* (see page 8).

Tunes marked with an asterisk (*) are included on the recording.

Paul de Grae

THE HARVEST HOME

Hornpipe.

This is almost too easy, but we have to start somewhere. Hornpipes generally sound best with a fairly simple steady backing, like the bass-string/chord alternation shown here, spiced up with the odd bass run. Drop-D tuning is used - as standard, except 6th string down to D. Play with a pick or thumb-and-fingers, as you prefer. If using a pick, try the different effects of playing the chord on the up-stroke and on the down-stroke; the bass is almost always a down-stroke. Also try damping the chord, that is, making it staccato by easing the pressure of your left-hand fingers as soon as the chord has been played; this is an element of the swing band style of guitar backing later adapted by Willie Johnson for Shetland music.

The Harvest Home is a simple enough tune, but its structure is typical of many of the more difficult tunes later in the book. So let's take a look at it. This is not just a classroom exercise, since a knowledge of where a tune is likely to go is very useful when you're accompanying an unfamiliar tune.

The first thing to notice is that the melody is in two parts, sometimes called 'the tune' and 'the turn', each eight bars long. The first part is played twice, then likewise the second, and then the whole lot is repeated as often as you like. Let's call these two parts A and B.

Next, each part is itself divisible into two four-bar phrases (A1 and A2, B1 and B2). In this case, as in many others, A1 and A2 are basically the same phrase with two different endings; while the second part begins with a new phrase (B1) and then ends the same as the first part (i.e. B2 is the same as A2).

The tune structure can be represented as:

A1 - A2 - A1 - A2 - B1 - A2 - B1 - A2
1st part   1st part   2nd part   2nd part

In some tunes, the second part may contain two new phrases, but still finish on the repeat with the end of the first part:

A1 - A2 - A1 - A2 - B1 - B2 - B1 - A2
1st part   1st part   2nd part   2nd part

Finally, the first and second parts may be quite independent:

A1 - A2 - A1 - A2 - B1 - B2 - B1 - B2
1st part   1st part   2nd part   2nd part

Many tunes have more than two parts, and other combinations are possible, but the vast majority of traditional Irish dance tunes follow one of these formats. To offset all that repetition, traditional musicians use a wide range of variation. For instance, the descending notes in the fourth bar of each part are much the same, but a traditional player would see this as an opportunity for some variation, so in the second part I have added more triplets. And a different ending is shown to each part, although they could be played the same.

FAR FROM HOME

Reel.

Here again the essence of the accompaniment is a bass-string/chord alternation, with some runs on the bass strings, and a few more chords this time; but since this is a reel, it is played faster than *The Harvest Home*. It's a fine lively tune, and you can have some fun with it. It sounds good in the key of A as well - see the solo version on page 66. Notice that this tune has exactly the same structure as the previous one.

Although this tune is in the key of G, drop-D tuning is used again for the sake of the extra power in the bass. The changes in chord fingering that this involves are described in Part 2. If you prefer to play in standard tuning, replace the low D notes with D on the open 4th string.

The G7 and C# diminished chords shown in brackets are optional variations to add a bit of pizzazz to the backing; otherwise, stay on the previous chord (G or C).

Many years after collecting this tune, O'Neill, a native of West Cork, recalled: 'When in California [in 1867] I picked up no. 1261 (Far From Home) from the whistling of a companion while herding a flock of 3,000 sheep on the plains at the foot of the Sierra Nevada range'. Far from home indeed.

OLD JOHN'S JIG (1) *   Jig.

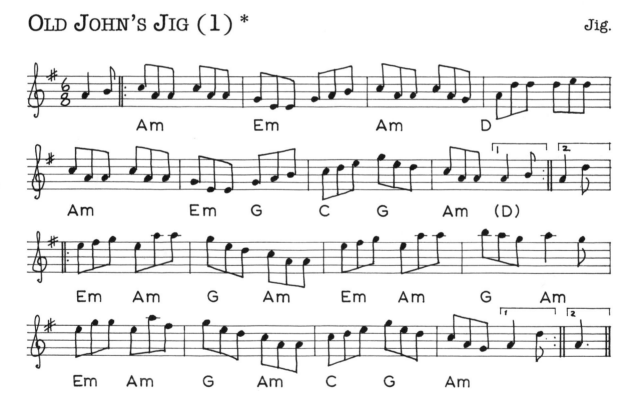

This tune has been recorded by, among others, Arty McGlynn, Tommy Peoples, and Paddy Glackin (paired with a reel version called *The Bank of Ireland*, on his album with Jolyon Jackson, 'Hidden Ground').

The accompaniment can be played in standard tuning, but sounds better in Irish tuning if you feel like trying it. Instead of strictly following the chords, try the Am/G chording described on page 18, with a fingering pattern moving up and down the middle strings, and drones on the outer strings.

CHORD SUBSTITUTION

We're not finished with *Old John's Jig* yet, because I want to use it to illustrate the concept of chord substitution - a way to develop a more interesting backing by replacing some of the obvious chords with other, more subtle ones.

You've met chord substitution already, in the backing to *Far From Home* - the E minor at the start of the second part replaces the more obvious G chord.

Because Irish music is not harmonic by nature, accompaniment chords must be deduced from the music. Typically, a part of the tune will contain some prominent notes that suggest a particular chord, as the opening of *The Harvest Home* suggests the chord of D, and the opening of *Old John's Jig* (containing the notes A and C) suggests the chord of A minor.

But at least three notes are needed to define a chord, and there are less obvious chords that also contain A and C. Add the note F and you get the chord of F major, or by adding D and F# you get D7. The latter is suggested by the habit common among pipers of sounding a D on the drones as an accompaniment to almost any tune, regardless of key (not always a good idea, I agree).

For each note of the scale, there is an obvious chord, and one or two less obvious ones which can be substituted. Look for parts of the tune where substitutions can be made without being too fussy; for example, it can be a good effect to use different chords for 'landmark' notes in repeated passages, so that the repeat is a development rather than mere repetition.

Below are the scales of G, D and A major and A and E minor, with chords shown for each note of the scale. The same principles apply to other keys. Major scales may have a flattened 7th note (F natural in the key of G, for example), and minor scales and harmonies get more complicated than major ones, hence the extra notes and chords shown. Bear in mind too that some tunes may require more exotic chords, to say nothing of the 9ths, 13ths, diminished and augmented chords that clever players might use.

		I	II	III	IV	V	VI	VII	VII
G major:	note	G	A	B	C	D	E	F	F#
	chord	G	D	G	C	D	Em	F	D
		Em	Am	Em	Am	G	C	Dm	Bm
		C	F	Bm	F	Bm	Am		
D major:	note	D	E	F#	G	A	B	C	C#
	chord	D	A	D	G	A	Bm	C	A
		Bm	Em	Bm	Em	D	G	Am	F#m
		G	C	F#m	C	F#m	Em		
A major:	note	A	B	C#	D	E	F#	G	G#
	chord	A	E	A	D	E	F#m	G	E
		F#m	Bm	F#m	Bm	A	D	Em	C#m
		D	G	C#m	G	C#m	Bm		

		I	II	III	IV	V	VI	VI	VII	VII
A minor:	note	A	B	C	D	E	F	F#	G	G#
	chord	Am	G	Am	G	Am	F	D	G	E
		F	E(m)	C	D(m)	C	Dm		C	
		D(m)		F		E(m)			Em	
E minor:	note	E	F#	G	A	B	C	C#	D	D#
	chord	Em	D	Em	D	Em	C	A	D	B
		C	B(m)	G	A(m)	G	Am		G	
		A(m)		C		B(m)			Bm	

31

SOME GENERAL TIPS ON CHORD SUBSTITUTION:

1. It can add drive to a tune to finish a part on the sub-dominant or IV-chord rather than the expected tonic or I- chord: for example, in a tune in the key of D, to use a G rather than a D. This seems to propel the tune forward into the next part.

2. A useful technique at the link between parts is to stay on a dominant or V-chord at the end of a part, where a tonic chord would be expected, incorporating a tonic *(doh)* note into the chord if necessary to avoid clashing with the melody. Again using the key of D as an example, that would mean staying on a chord of A instead of changing to a D chord at the end of a part - an A chord with a D note in it (A4 or A11), or at least without a C# note (A~), which would probably clash with the melody.

3. Occasionally substitute a minor chord for its relative major (E minor for G, B minor for D, F# minor for A, etc.).

4. Use passing chords. The most common passing chords are: in major keys, a chord based on the II note of the scale, leading to a chord based on the V; and in minor keys, a chord based on the IV note of the scale, leading to a chord based on the VII. For example, when changing from G to D, insert an A or A7 before the D; or when changing from A minor to G, insert a D or D7 before the G. These passing chords are played only briefly, but they add a certain quality to the accompaniment.

5. Sometimes the trend of the tune will suggest a chord sequence that appears to contradict the actual notes; thus, in many tunes the closing phrase, whatever the notes it contains, will call for the chords V-I or dominant-tonic (in the key of D, an A chord followed by a D). Likewise, in the first part of *McFadden's Handsome Daughter* (page 79), the D and E4 chords technically don't fit the notes of the melody, yet they have a flow of their own (I hope).

6. Try more complex chords such as the 9ths and 11ths shown in Part 2.

7. Experiment with discords (bum notes to the ignorant). There are no absolute rules about these things - what is intolerable to one person may be perfectly acceptable to another. The important thing is to recognise the dramatic power of discords: they impart a tension to the tune which is resolved by passing on to a more restful harmony, and they give variety. Playing an F note or chord against an E in the melody could be a fairly nasty clash, but I hope you like the effect of this discord in the backing to *The Humours of Tullycrine* on page 34.

OLD JOHN'S JIG (2) *

Jig.

So let's look at this tune again, this time with different chords (inspired by Jolyon Jackson's arrangement on 'Hidden Ground'), and a counter-melody in the second part. The counter-melody need not be followed strictly - it's merely a sketch of some ideas you might use as an alternative to chords. The effect of changing the chords gives a different colour to the piece, and shows the power an accompanist can have in highlighting the nuances of a tune and bringing out hidden harmonies.

On the recording, this tune is played four times, the first two times using the chords of version (1), and then with the chords and counter-melody of version (2).

THE HUMOURS OF TULLYCRINE*

Hornpipe.

TUNING : D · A · D · E · A · E

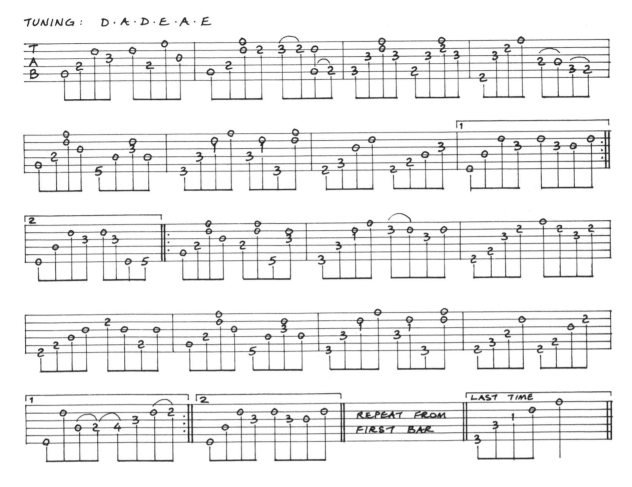

This is played in an even rhythm, rather than the dotted rhythm of most hornpipes. The fingerstyle accompaniment is arranged for Irish tuning; you'll find it easier to use the tablature until you're familiar with the tuning. Chords for standard tuning (or better, drop-D) are also shown; the F major 7th chord is just like a standard F but with an open first string.

The main harmonic interest is in the bass notes, which should be allowed to ring on where possible, and the open 1st and 2nd strings should also resonate throughout much of the tune. Open strings are marked '0' on the staff notation.

The left-hand fingering is straightforward enough. I use my left thumb for some 6th string notes, but it's only fair to mention that this habit is frowned upon by classical guitar teachers, as it moves the left hand from its ideal position.

As for right-hand fingering, the first note of each group of four is, as you would expect, played by the thumb, but generally the second note is also played with the thumb, which gives a certain texture to the accompaniment. Thumb notes are shown with stems pointing down; first and second fingers will do for the others.

Notice the effect of the D chords and the F major 7th (an F chord with an added E note). These form part of a downward bass line, A-G-F-E-D, which turns up to F instead of down to D at the end. Each of those F and D chords is an example of chord substitution, in place of the more obvious A minor chord.

On the recording, this arrangement is preceded by a slow air version on solo electric guitar, using a free adaptation of the hornpipe melody. Playing dance tunes as slow airs, or vice versa, is not as odd as it may seem; for example, the well-known jig *The Gallowglass* was originally a slow air called *Nathaniel Gow's Lament for the Death of his Brother*.

I learned this tune from the Kevin Burke album 'If the cap fits' (Green Linnet 3009), where it's called *Bobby Casey's Hornpipe*. Mícheál Ó Domhnaill plays lovely backing guitar. Mícheál Ó Domhnaill, incidentally, is a master of the chord substitution techniques discussed earlier - listen to his great album with Kevin Burke, 'Portland' (Green Linnet 1041), arguably the best example of guitar accompaniment in traditional Irish music on record (but then, so is Arty McGlynn's work on the Patrick Street albums...).

THE NEW-MOWN MEADOWS *

Reel

MISS MONAGHAN *

Reel

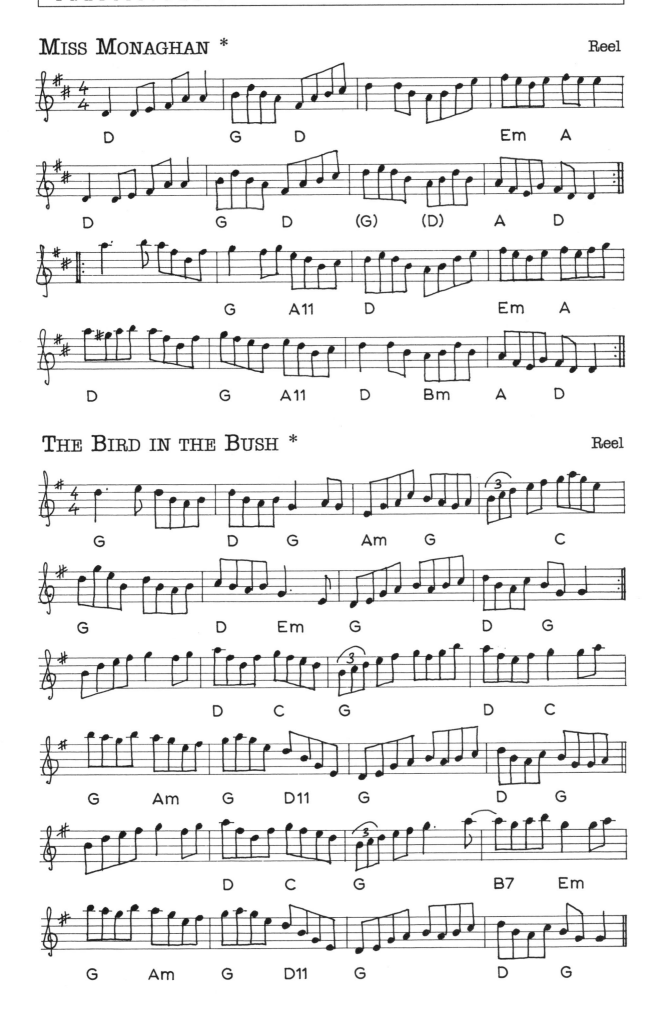

THE BIRD IN THE BUSH *

Reel

The New-Mown Meadows is from the accordion playing of Séamus Begley, whose combination with Steve Cooney on guitar is one of the most exciting duos I've ever heard. It's commonly played a tone lower, as Denis Murphy and Julia Clifford play it on 'Kerry Fiddles' (Topic/Ossian OSS(CD)10).

Miss Monaghan is the first reel I learned, from The Johnstons' eponymous (always wanted to work that word in somewhere) album, recorded in 1968, with Mick Moloney on banjo and Paul Brady on guitar. The tune re-emerged from the mists of memory recently, and the change into *The Bird in the Bush* happened spontaneously at a session in Tralee, when Kate Mulcahy and Kevin Ryan (fiddles) launched straight into it as if it had been rehearsed - the sort of telepathy that often occurs at sessions. Cape Breton guitarist Dave MacIsaac plays *Miss Monaghan* on his 'Nimble Fingers' album.

The Bird in the Bush is a well-known tune which seems to have escaped O'Neill's attention - perhaps it's a later composition. Michael Coleman's version is transcribed in "Bowing Styles in Irish Fiddle Playing" by David Lyth (Comhaltas Ceoltóirí Éireann, 1981). Jackie Daly plays it in hornpipe time with an interesting variant, *The Two Birds in the Bush* (CRÉ II 232), on his album with Seamus Creagh. Notice the chord substitution in this arrangement. I like the B7 leading to E minor in the second part, myself.

Standard tuning is fine for these tunes, but drop-D works better; Irish tuning is used on the recording. Chords shown in brackets are optional variations. Don't be alarmed by the A11 in the second tune - if you look back at Part 2, you'll see it's an easy chord in either tuning.

WALSH'S HORNPIPE *

Hornpipe.

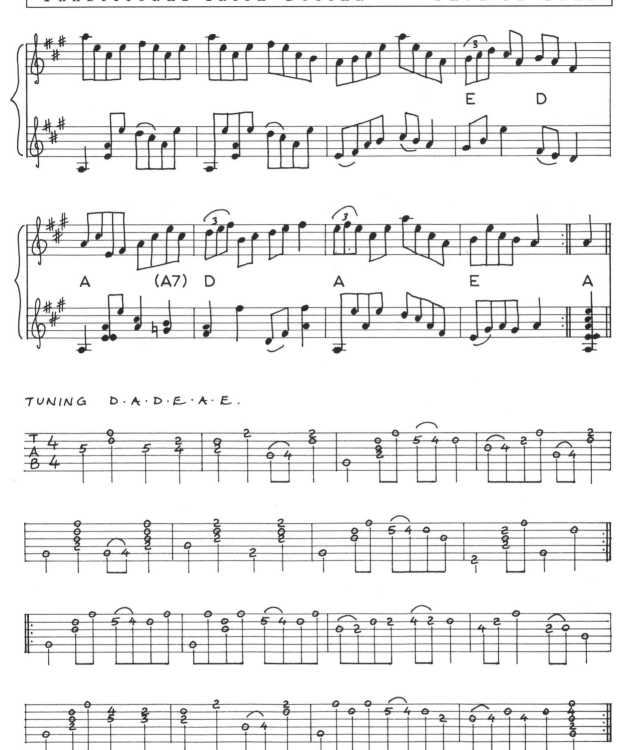

TUNING D·A·D·E·A·E.

This was a favourite of the late Ned Nolan of Ardrahan, near Ardfert, County Kerry, a fine fiddler and a lovely man with whom my friends and I used to play regularly. It was recorded by Kevin Burke and Mícheál Ó Domhnaill on 'Promenade' (Green Linnet 3010), and is also in Sarah McQuaid's 'The Irish DADGAD Guitar Book'.

The accompaniment is played in Irish tuning in a gentle flat-picking style, with occasional counter-melodies and much use of the open 1st and 2nd strings. The notation shows the general idea, but you don't need to follow it too strictly; for example, you would probably use more bass notes the second time around. If using standard tuning, follow the chords under the melody line.

THE RETURN OF SPRING

Polka

THE MOUNTAIN PATHWAY

Polka

Unlike jigs, reels and hornpipes, polka tunes are still closely associated with dancing, and the best way to learn to play polkas is to get some experience playing for dancers, or better again, learn the dances yourself. Next best is to listen to musicians who are used to playing for set dancers, for example, Johnny O'Leary, Denis Murphy, Julia Clifford, Jackie Daly, Noel Hill, Tony McMahon, Denis Doody, etc.; recordings of all these musicians are readily available.

A simple bass/chord alternation, with the occasional bass run, is suitable for these polkas. Keep the rhythm strong and steady, and try damping the chords by relaxing your left-hand fingers slightly as soon as you've played the chord. Drop-D tuning is recommended. You could play in standard tuning, but the loss of the bass D would be a pity. See Part 2 for chord shapes in drop-D, and for the G diminished chord in the second tune.

These polkas are from the playing of the great James Morrison, and can be heard on an album of recordings he made with the piper Tom Ennis in the 1930s, re-issued by Topic (12 TS 390).

THE LOWDOWN JIG

Jig

CONNIE O'CONNELL'S JIG

Jig

The first tune had no name when I learned it (from Kate Mulcahy) and *The Lowdown* is simply an obvious nickname that has stuck, at least in this area. It's called *A Bush on the Hill* in 'Brenda Stubbert's Collection of Fiddle Tunes' (Cranford Publications, Cape Breton), and on the recording by Kevin and Liz Carroll ('Fathers and Daughters', Shanachie 79054) it's called *The Bush on the Hill* and is credited to the fiddler Brendan McGlinchey. On the other hand, Brendan McGlinchey himself says he doesn't know who wrote it, and thinks it may be one of several tunes that came over from America after Ciarán Mac Mathúna's collecting trips there in the early 1960s.

The second tune is named after the well-known fiddle player from West Cork, and was recorded by Jackie Daly and Seamus Creagh on their classic Gael Linn album (057). It was also recorded by Joe Ryan and Eddie Clark on "Crossroads" (Green Linnet 1030) as *The Two-and-Sixpenny girl*.

The accompaniment is for guitar in Irish tuning, capoed at the 5th fret, using key-of-D chord shapes. Fret numbers are counted up from the capo position, so '0' for open string is actually the fifth fret. Rather than a full written backing, the tablature shows some of the various chord shapes which can be used, plus one or two little runs. There are touches of syncopation in *Connie O'Connell's* - playing the chord a little ahead of the beat, for example at the end of bar 1, where the last chord 'belongs' at the start of bar 2. Otherwise the strumming pattern is up to yourself. At the end of the repeat of the second part of *Connie O'Connell's*, there is a section where the 5th, 2nd and 1st strings are played open while a two finger chord pattern moves along the 4th and 3rd strings. This sort of thing is very handy in Irish tuning, and sounds really good.

Chords for standard tuning with no capo are shown under the melody line; these don't necessarily correspond to the Irish tuning chords.

THE SILVER SPIRE

Reel

I'M WAITING FOR YOU

Reel

THE SILVER SPEAR

Reel

The Silver Spire comes from the playing of Dingle accordionist Maurice McKenna. On Dave MacIsaac's 'Nimble Fingers' album, it's called *The Great Eastern*, and is credited to one Clem Titus. The tune itself is a good way of practicing scales and arpeggios, and shows that practice doesn't have to be boring. Here again the repeat of the second part has been written out with alternative chords, and some variations in the melody while we're at it.

I learned the second tune at sessions here in Kerry. Who is waiting for whom? and why?

The Silver Spear is common throughout Ireland, and it would be hard to find a traditional musician who didn't have some version of it (although, like *The Bird in the Bush*, it's not in the O'Neill collections). The variation in the repeat of the first part is lifted from Kevin Burke. Compare the second part with that of *The New-mown Meadows* (also called *The Old 'Silver Spear'*) on page 36. See Part 2 for the A9 chord.

THE CHANCELLOR

Hornpipe

PETER WYPER'S HORNPIPE

Hornpipe

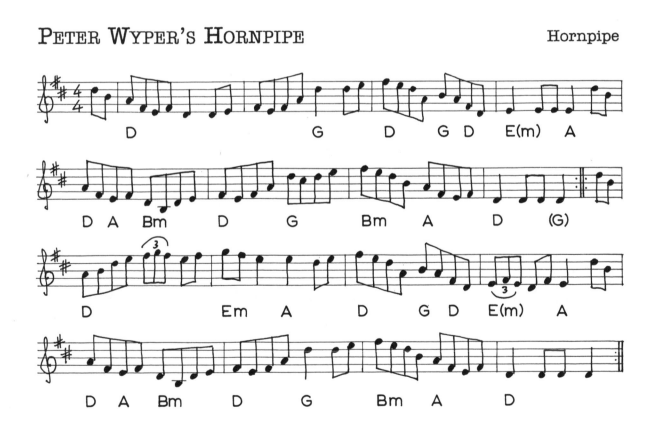

These tunes come from the playing of Paddy O'Sullivan, one of the last of the once-numerous fiddlers playing in the distinct regional style of North Kerry. Paddy has the ability to make even well-known tunes sound fresh, but he also has a great repertoire of unusual tunes, such as these two hornpipes and the two jigs on pages 63 & 64.

The Chancellor is Paddy's version of the tune which O'Neill calls *The Humours of Ballinlass*. O'Neill's setting is in G, whereas Paddy's is in the brighter key of A. *Breen's Hornpipe*, played by Martin Mulvihill, is very similar, and Paddy Taylor's *Loughill Hornpipe* is also closely related.

Peter Wyper was a famous Scottish melodeon player of the early part of this century, and made many 78rpm recordings, either solo or with his brother Daniel, and with Peter's son James on piano. Daniel spent his honeymoon in Ireland, returning several times, and included some Irish tunes in his repertoire (my thanks to Máire O'Keeffe and to Glenn Cumiskey of the Irish Traditional Music Archive for information on the Wyper brothers).

The quick chord changes in both these tunes (Bm-A-Bm and D-A-Bm) can be replaced by bass notes for variety: B-A-B and D-C#-B, respectively.

HARDY MAN THE FIDDLER *

Slip jig

MOLL ROE *

Slip jig

A   E   A   D   A   E   F#m E   D   A

A   Bm E   A   (Bm) D   A   D   E   F#m E   A   A

The 9/8 timing of slip jigs makes an attractive contrast to the more common jigs and reels. Accompanying such tunes can take some getting used to - especially if players shift from the usual 6/8 jig into a slip jig, as sometimes happens.

A slight jazz tinge in the accompaniment seems to suit slip jigs. The natural accents fall on the 1st, 4th and 7th beats, but a little syncopation is effective. Try an accented bass note on the 1st note of the bar, skip the 2nd beat, and play an accented chord on the 3rd beat - bringing forward the accent that would otherwise fall on the 4th - and continue with less strong strumming for the remainder of the bar. The accent on the 7th beat is optional unless there's a chord change at that point, in which case it's a strong accent:

1   (2)   **3**   4   5   6   (**7**)   8   9

bass   chord   ....syncopated strum....................

The first tune is sometimes called *Hardiman the Fiddler*, but if there was once such a person, his or her fame has not lasted. I've used O'Neill's spelling. Sarah McQuaid includes this tune in her DADGAD book. The harmony for the second part of the tune is optional, and is handy enough in Irish tuning, DADGAD, or drop-D.

Moll Roe, played here in the key of A, is in G in O'Neill and in D in Breathnach (see Part 5). I heard it first as the air to 'The Devil and Bailiff McGlynn', sung by the wondrous June Tabor on 'Ashes and Diamonds' (Shanachie 79055). 'Moll Roe', or 'Red Mary', is also the title of a song, one of the many songs and stories about the redoubtable 17th century lady Máire Ruadh Ní Mahon, thrice-married chatelaine of Leamaneh Castle in County Clare, whose impressive remains stand beside the road from Ennis up to The Burren (the castle's remains, that is, not Máire Ruadh's). See Breathnach's notes in 'Ceol Rince na hÉireann II', and also a brief history of the castle in 'The Houses of Ireland' by Brian de Breffny and Rosemary ffolliott (Thames & Hudson, 1975).

AGGIE WHITE'S REEL *(comp. Paddy Kelly)

Reel.

I learned this tune, and many others, at the regular Tuesday night session in Baily's Corner, Tralee, and as is often the case with tunes learned at sessions, it came without a name. Breathnach's setting (also untitled) is from the fiddle playing of Aggie White. It has been recorded by Fisherstreet as *Aggie White's* on 'Out in the Night' (Mulligan 057), and by Carl Hession on 'Ceol Inné Ceol Inniu' (Gael Linn 173), where it is credited to Paddy Kelly.

On the recording, the backing guitar is capoed at the fifth fret and key-of-D chord shapes are used, as shown in the lower row of chords. Chords for guitar without capo are shown directly under the melody - a bass D would be nice if no capo is used, so try drop-D, DADGAD or Irish tuning.

THE HUMOURS OF GLANDART

Jig

MUNSTER BUTTERMILK

Jig

The *Humours of Glandart* is usually played in the key of D, although Josephine Marsh also plays it down low on her highly recommendable album (JM MC 001). To play in D, either move all the chords up a fourth (A to D, etc.), or put a capo on the 5th fret and use the chords shown. Try working out a harmony for the second part, along the lines of that used on *Hardy Man the Fiddler*. Glandart is in west Cork, not far from Francis O'Neill's birthplace, Tralibane.

The second tune was memorably recorded by Denis Murphy and Julia Clifford on 'The Star above the Garter' (Claddagh CC5). *Munster Buttermilk* is the Sliabh Luachra name for the tune which Breathnach calls *The Sports of Multyfarnham*, while just to confuse matters, the tune which Breathnach calls *Munster Buttermilk* is more generally known as *Behind the Haystack*. All clear as mud? Sarah McQuaid has a duet version in 'The Irish DADGAD Guitar Book'.

THE DRUNKEN LANDLADY *   Reel

UP THE TRACK * (comp. Joe Thoma)   Reel

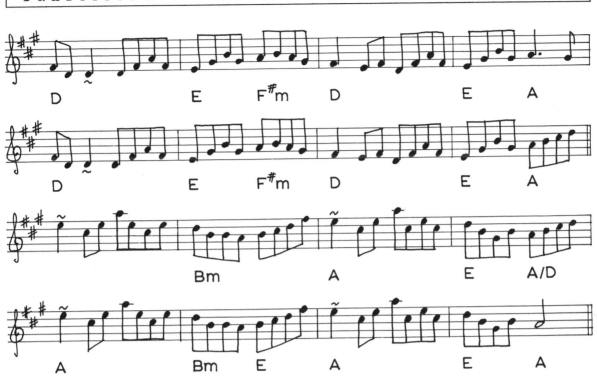

The title of a tune is generally no more than a tag to remember it by. If it's a personal name it usually refers to a player associated with the tune (*Walsh's Hornpipe*) or occasionally the composer (*O'Dowd's No. 9*). But, as Breandán Breathnach commented, 'It is nonsense to suppose that *The Irish Washerwoman* in some mystical manner represents the strange personality of that now ancient lady, or that one may determine on hearing *The Mason's Apron* whether a stonemason's apron or a Freemason's apron is implied by the title'.

So don't ask who the drunken landlady was; I don't know. I learned the tune from the classic album by Noel Hill and Tony Linnane (Tara 2006). Tommy Peoples' version is in his book and tape 'Fifty Irish Fiddle Tunes' (Waltons, Dublin, 1986).

Up the Track is by Joe Thoma, a fine fiddle player and Kenmare's answer to Cecil B. de Mille (the Cibeal Arts Festival, of which Joe is prime mover, involves a cast of thousands). It's on a cassette which Joe made in 1986 called 'Up the Track', recorded at the aforesaid house on the hill, outside Kenmare; Donagh Long played guitar and co-produced the album with Joe.

On the recording, both guitars are capoed at the second fret, so the tunes come out in actual F# minor and B major respectively. The backing to the second tune uses partial chords on the middle strings over a recurring bass A, as described in Part 2.

THE STRAYAWAY CHILD

Jig.

Learned from the fiddle playing of my late friend Tom McCarthy of Ardfert, County Kerry, who learned it in London in the 1950s. This elaborate jig is always attributed to Michael Gorman, although broadcaster and musical historian Harry Bradshaw told me that Gorman himself referred to it as 'one of Margaret [Barry]'s compositions'. Whether because of its length or its difficulty, the tune initially didn't catch on, and Jimmy Power is the only one whom Tom remembered playing it in London. Since then, it has gained wider circulation in Kevin Burke's version with The Bothy Band on 'Out of the wind and into the sun' (Green Linnet 3013).

For variety and ease of playing, some of the rapid chord changes can be done simply as bass notes.

Tom McCarthy. Photo: Ciarán Dalton

PART 4: SOLO TUNES

Solo playing is the purest form of traditional music, and also the most personal. There is something paradoxical about that, when you think of it. Traditional music, like folk culture in general, is an art based in the community, and its style and content are evolved communally; yet at the peak of its expression it is literally in the hands of an individual, and is created afresh at each performance (for music, unlike the visual arts, has no existence except in the performance - staff notation is not itself music). The notes of the melody provide a framework on which the individual musician constructs his or her own interpretation, and two of the most important creative tools are *variation* and *ornamentation*.

VARIATION

There are examples of variation in many of the accompanied tunes, and it should by now be apparent that a printed setting is not sacred: in any tune there will be bits which can be played in a variety of ways without losing the overall identity, and this should be remembered when learning tunes from books, including this one.

Like improvisation, variation cannot readily be taught, but as you grow into the music, it should come naturally. On page 59 the jig *Father O'Flynn* has been deconstructed to show some typical tricks of variation, and all the other solo tunes include some variations.

ORNAMENTATION

Ornamentation in this context means adding grace notes - quick little extra notes - to the tune, and is influenced by the instrument being played: fiddlers don't use the same ornaments as pipers, for example. Also, the choice of ornament depends to some extent on the note being ornamented: a fiddler will use different ornaments for open-string and fingered notes.

The tunes in this book are mostly presented without written ornamentation. This makes them easier to read, but also means you can ornament the tune according to your own taste. So much depends on phrasing and individual or regional style that it would be misleading to lay down any general rules. Naturally there is no traditional method of ornamentation for guitar, as there is for established traditional instruments (see the chapter on 'Traditional Techniques and Styles' in Breathnach's 'Folk Music and Dances of Ireland'). But traditional decorations such as rolls and triplets can readily be played on the guitar, and can be used along with other techniques such as partial chords and bass notes which are not available to players of more traditional instruments (except to some extent accordionists and pipers).

The techniques can be divided into those done with the left hand and those done with the right (my apologies to left-handed players - please reverse left and right throughout).

LEFT-HAND TECHNIQUES

The simplest left-hand techniques are the *hammer-on* and the *pull-off*. As if you didn't already know, to hammer-on means to fret a higher note after picking a lower one, and the pull-off is the reverse of this, taking your fretting finger away to sound the lower note, either on an open string or fretted by another finger (preferably your own).

As well as smoothing the flow of the melody, hammer-on and pull-off can be used for individual grace notes (indicated by a little quaver with a line through its tail) - in the example, to separate two notes of the same pitch

Example 1

The grace note is short, flicking rapidly onto the main note, and is usually a higher note; thus the pull-off is more often used than the hammer-on. If you want to be posh, you can call the grace note by its resounding classical name, *acciaccatura*.

Hammer-on and pull-off are combined for the *triplet*, which consists of three notes played in the time of two. The first note is picked by the right hand, followed quickly by either a hammer-on and pull-off (upward triplet) or a pull-off and hammer-on (downward triplet), finishing on the first note. *Example 2* shows an upward triplet, and *Example 3* a downward triplet.

Example 2   *Example 3*

As well as ornamenting individual notes, triplets can be used to fill between notes. Examples of this can be found in many of the tunes on the following pages.

The *roll* is more tricky, consisting of three grace notes wrapped around the main note; all can be played off one pick stroke, using a combination of hammer-on and pull-off. *Example 4* shows a few typical rolls.

Example 4

Another traditional form of ornamentation is the *crann* (*Example 5*), originally a piper's technique but also used by virtuosi of other instruments. Two, three or even four grace notes are scattered in between repeated main notes, and it's a point of honour not to play two consecutive grace notes the same. Personally I think it's more trouble than it's worth trying to do this sort of thing on guitar, which doesn't have the sustain of the pipes, but by all means try it and prove me wrong.

Example 5

Two other left-hand techniques are the *slide* and the *bend*. These are simple enough, and respectively mean sliding your finger rapidly up to the note from a fret or more below, and changing the pitch of a fretted note by pushing up or down with your fretting finger. The effect in either case is to smooth the approach to a note and to assist the flow of the tune; the bend is a particularly good way to play 'lonesome' notes (see page 90).

Finally, *vibrato*: this could be described as a series of quick little bends, minutely changing the pitch of the main note. It is done by shaking your fretting finger back and forth either parallel to the string or at right angles to it. Vibrato is foreign to Irish traditional music and should be used sparingly, if at all.

RIGHT-HAND TECHNIQUES

You can use separate pick stokes for the triplets and rolls described above, rather than plucking some of the notes with your left-hand fingers. Another type of triplet, which can only be picked, is the *trill*, consisting of three identical notes played in rapid succession. For comparison, try the opening of *The New-mown Meadows*, first with a downward triplet, then an upward triplet, then a trill, and finally a roll (notice also the single grace note separating the first two E notes). The grace notes may be picked or partly played with the left hand.

Example 6

Each of these has a different effect, and each can be equally valid.

Other tricks include striking an open string while playing the melody on an adjacent string, playing the occasional bass note in gaps in the tune, and playing full or partial chords here and there.

FATHER O'FLYNN*

Jig.

Here are two settings of this well-known jig. Above is the basic tune, with accompanying chords. The next two pages show the version on the recording, where the tune is played three times. The first run through the tune has been transcribed; as is customary, this is a relatively simple rendering. On the second and third times around, more variations are added, and these are written out separately underneath - all fairly simple tricks, ranging from simply altering or omitting one note to changing whole bars, which can be applied to any tune you want to play. Tablature is for guitar in Irish tuning.

O'Neill calls this tune *The Top of Cork Road*, but it's better known by the title of the song set to it by Reverend Alfred Perceval Graves (father of the poet Robert Graves). The tune dates back at least to 1770: O'Neill mentions it as being in print at that date.

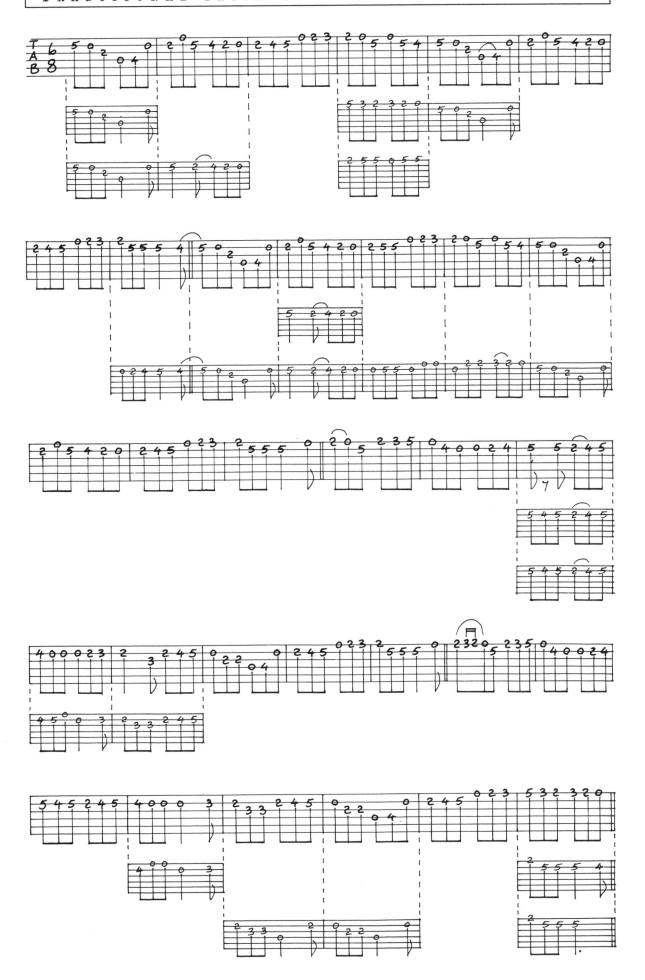

A final word on ornamentation: don't forget the power of simplicity. A few notes played well are much better than a show-off display of super-fast picking; and sometimes even silence can be an ornament - listen to the stopped notes and little pauses on any recording of Micho Russell. The ornamentation is meant to serve the tune, not the other way around. Just put some thought into it, and avoid the two extremes of excessively bare, colourless playing, and the sort of overkill which spoils the melody, and you'll be right. End of sermon.

There are literally thousands of Irish traditional dance tunes, of which the following are a small selection which work particularly well on guitar. Except for *The Moving Cloud*, which is in drop-D, the tablature is for Irish tuning, but you can use other tunings without much bother. Flat-picking is recommended for all these tunes: in my experience, fingerpicking doesn't give you enough speed, although again *The Moving Cloud* is the exception - I play it fingerstyle on the recording.

In the tablature, notes which are hammered-on or pulled off are linked by a slur line ($\frown$); in some cases, a decoration is written out, more often a decorated note is indicated by a squiggle over it ($\sim$). These phrasing marks are entirely optional.

If you're playing with other musicians, try playing the melody once or twice, and then take more of an accompanist's role in the later repeats. This varies the group sound and gives the melody players something to lean on. Chords are indicated for accompanying most of the solo tunes; these are merely an outline, which you can fill out by incorporating snatches of the tune, by varying the bass note of the chords, and so on.

THE BEES IN THE HEATHER *

Jig

PADDY O'SULLIVAN'S JIG *

Jig

Two unusual tunes from Paddy O'Sullivan (see also page 47), neither of which is in any of the major collections. I've heard other North Kerry fiddlers play the first tune, but the second seems to be unique to Paddy. Tablature is for Irish tuning.

Paddy O'Sullivan. Photo: Ciarán Dalton

FAR FROM HOME

Reel

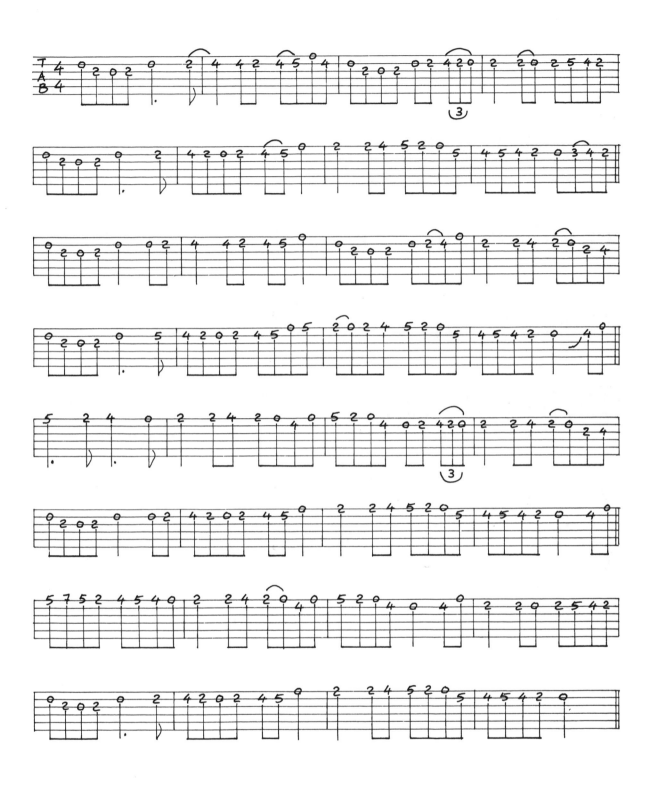

LAINGTON'S REEL

Reel

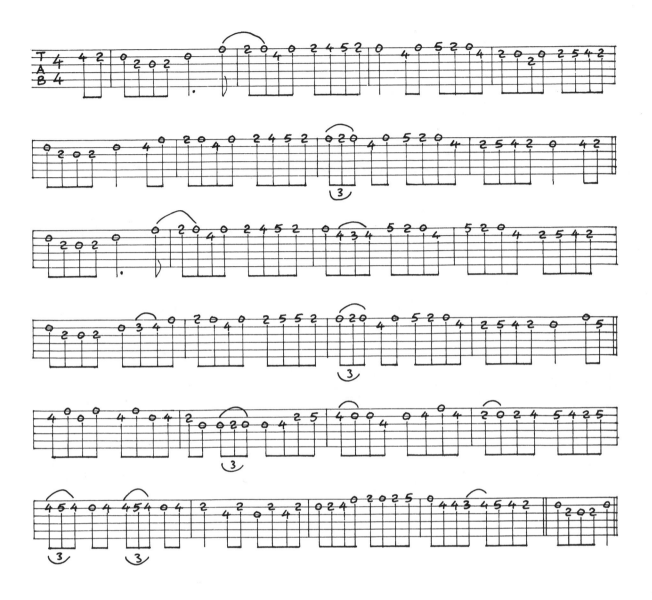

Far from Home is more usually played in G, as on page 28, but also sounds good up in A. Cape Breton fiddler Howie MacDonald plays it in both keys on his album 'The Ceilidh Trail' (Atlantica ATL 0193). Repeats are written out to show variations, and the chord sequence has been re- arranged this time.

Laington's Reel has exactly the same opening notes as *Far from Home*, which can cause confusion at sessions. Note that the first part is repeated, but not the second. The title is from the version played by Kevin Burke and Jackie Daly on 'If the cap fits' (Green Linnet 3009). Breathnach has two settings, one untitled and one called *Dillon Brown*, but this is not the same as O'Neill's *Dillon Brown*.

JACKY TAR *

Hornpipe

TUNING   E·A·D·E·A·E.

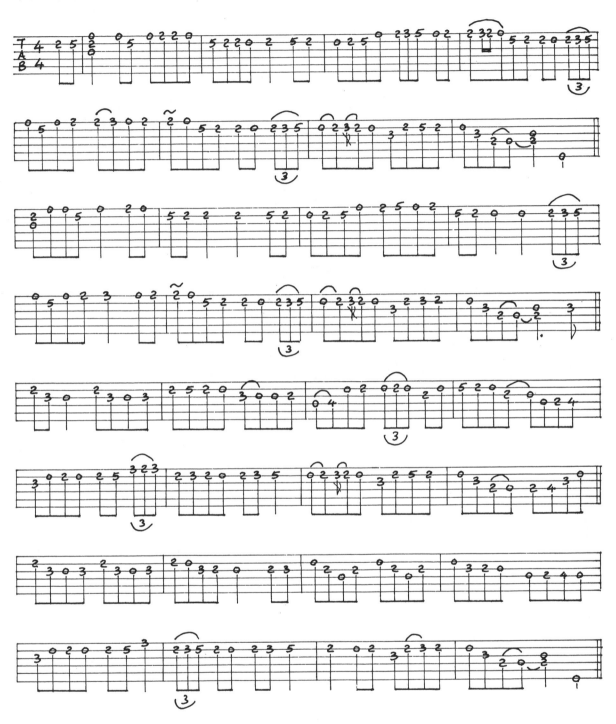

An open-string bass 'doh' is handy for the first tune, which is in E minor, so try a variant of Irish tuning, with the 6th string back up to E - EADEAE.

Nic Jones is one of my favourites as a singer and guitarist, but it was on the fiddle that he played *Jacky Tar* on 'The Noah's Ark Trap' (Shanachie 790003). It's a variant of the more widely known *Cuckoo's Nest*, which Breathnach says is itself a variant of an early Elizabethan bawdy song called *Come Ashore, Jolly Tar, and your Trousers on*. Devotees of bawdy songs will not need to be told what 'the cuckoo's nest' is a euphemism for.

THE FLOWERS OF EDINBURGH *

Hornpipe

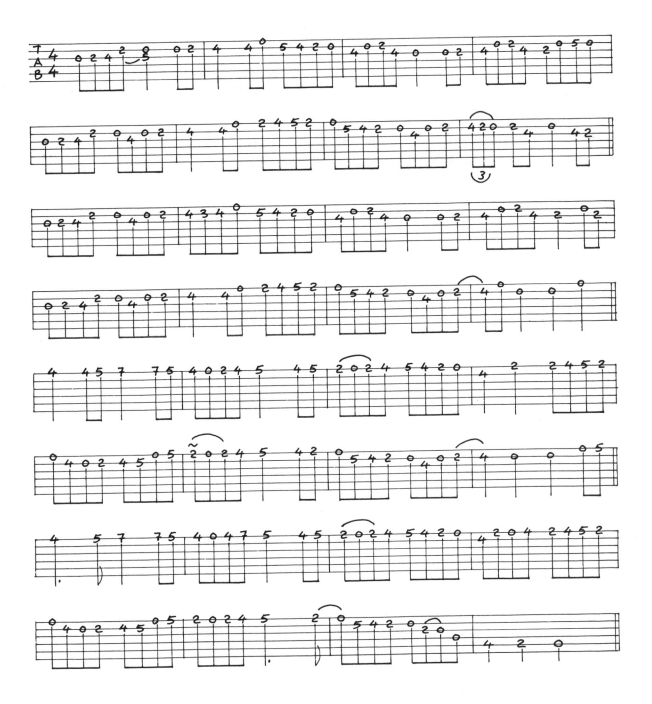

The *Flowers of Edinburgh* is a well-known tune, but this setting has an attractive variation in the opening bar of each part, learned from the playing of Peter Ostroushko and Bertram Levy on 'First Generation' (Flying Fish 392) - thanks to Ciarán Dalton for the loan of the album. The more usual version is in O'Neill.

THE MOVING CLOUD * (comp. Neilie Boyle)

Reel.

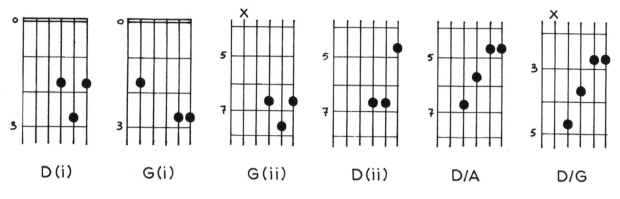

D(i)   G(i)   G(ii)   D(ii)   D/A   D/G

INTRO.   D(i) - G(i) - D(i) - G(ii) - D(ii) - G(ii) - D(ii) - D/A - D/G

TUNING: D·A·D·G·B·E (DROP-D).

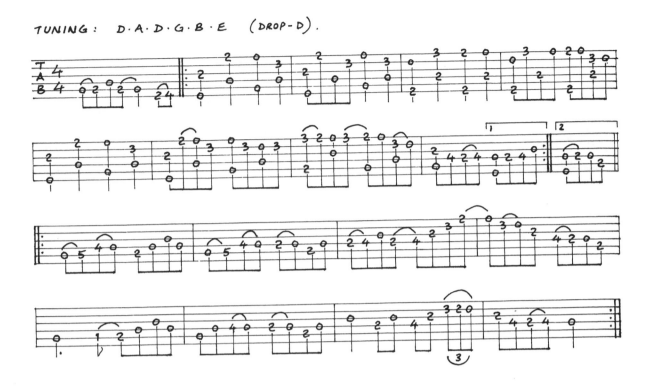

As usually played, this is a virtuoso display piece in G or F with three or even more parts, but the two-part version in D which I heard played by Paul Brock (accordion), Maeve Donnelly (fiddle), and Garry Ó Briain (mando-cello) seemed to bring out different qualities in the tune besides the show-off stuff - which I can't play anyway.

That version is the basis of this setting for fingerstyle guitar in drop-D tuning. The improvised introduction (the product of a so far unsuccessful attempt to combine *The Moving Cloud* with Pete Seeger's *Living in the Country*) is in a simple fingerpicking style - alternating bass notes on the beat, played by the thumb, with high notes played by the fingers scattered in between and sometimes on the beats. Using the chord shapes and listening to the recording, you should be able to work it out.

After the introduction, the usual second part of the tune is played first, and the alternating bass pattern continues. The usual first part (here played second) uses more of the lower strings, and it gets harder to keep the bass pattern going - which is why, on the recording, the accompaniment comes in at this point! Since there are fewer notes in the higher part of the tune, feel free to use ornamentation and variation to keep it interesting.

By leaving out the bass line, this setting can be played with a pick if you prefer. The higher part is good practice for cross-picking.

SONNY RIORDAN'S POLKA *

Polka

THE LAST OF JUNE (JENNY LIND) *

Polka

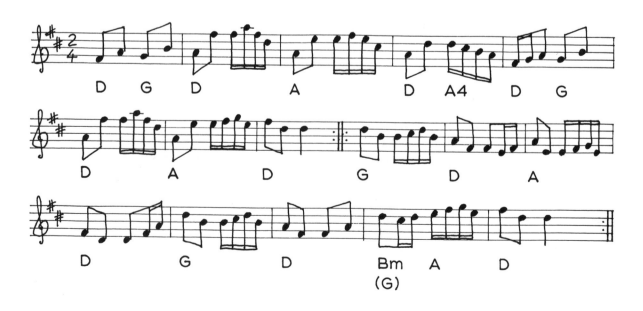

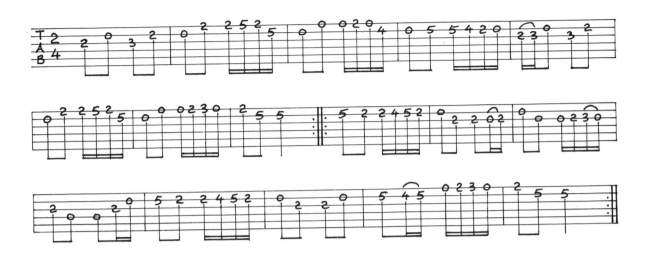

The polka, as a dance and as a tune, is found in various parts of Ireland, but is especially associated with the area of east Kerry and west Cork called Sliabh Luachra ('the rushy mountain'). The first of these tunes was collected by Máire O'Keeffe from Sonny Riordan of Tureencahill in Sliabh Luachra, who was a pupil of the great fiddle master Pádraig O'Keeffe.

The second tune is from the fiddle playing of Rose Murphy on a wonderful album called 'Milltown Lass' (Topic/Ossian OSS-21), and is a version of the well-known *Jenny Lind*. Jenny Lind (1820-1887) was a superstar opera singer, Sweden's greatest musical export apart from Abba. 'The Swedish Nightingale', as she was known, attracted huge crowds wherever she performed (including Dublin in 1846). Several composers named tunes in her honour, of which the best known today is The New Jenny Lind Polka by Wallerstein. It's interesting to compare this with Rose Murphy's traditional style version, which is in the more accessible key of D rather than the original F. It doesn't change key in the second part, nor does it venture into the high octave, but it is clearly the same tune, and to me, her variations sound more classically elegant than the original.

In writing out both tunes, the little link notes between parts have been omitted; you can guess these by now, I'm sure.

THE NEW JENNY LIND POLKA.
COMPOSED BY WALLERSTEIN

Camden Town was an important centre for Irish music in London in the 1950s and 1960s, a time when great players such as Bobby Casey, Jimmy Power, John and Julia Clifford, Lucy Farr, Con Curtin, Roger Sherlock, and many others were in full swing (hear, for example, the album 'Paddy in the Smoke', Topic 12T176/Ossian OSS 19). I had seen *Return to Camden Town* in Bulmer & Sharpley*'s* collection of tunes, and hadn't thought much of it until hearing it at a session in Belharbour, County Clare, when I realised it was a grand tune altogether. Later I tried a few bars of it on Con Curtin (now living in Brosna, County Kerry), and was rewarded with a superb rendition, none the worse for his not having played it in 25 years. So the moral of the story is: don't rely on books alone, but try to hear the tunes played by a good musician - no slight intended, incidentally, on Bulmer & Sharpley's excellent books.

Return to Camden Town has been recorded by Martin Carthy (inventor of 'Irish' tuning) and Dave Swarbrick on 'Skin and Bone' (Special Delivery SPD 1046), by Josephine Marsh on her solo album (JM MC 001), and by Mark Crickard (fiddle) and Donogh Hennessy (guitar) on a cassette called 'The Hurricane'.

John McFadden was a fiddler from whom O'Neill got many fine tunes, some composed by McFadden himself. He is pictured in "Irish Minstrels and Musicians" sitting beside another great O'Neill source, the piper James Early (in "The Dance Music of Ireland" their names are transposed in the caption). Unfortunately for your curiosity and mine, no picture of the handsome daughter appears.

I learned *O'Dowd's No. 9* from the elegant fiddle playing of Máire O'Keeffe. It was composed by John O'Dowd from Sligo, and over the years it has become very popular - in contrast to its stablemates, *O'Dowd's 1-8*, which I don't recall ever being mentioned, never mind played (*O'Dowd's Favourite*, an elaborate tune in G minor, may or may not be one of the missing eight).

Chords shown are for guitar without capo. On the recording, the backing guitar is capoed at the fifth fret for the first and third tunes, and at the seventh fret for the middle tune.

John McFadden   Sergt. James Early

RETURN TO CAMDEN TOWN *

Reel

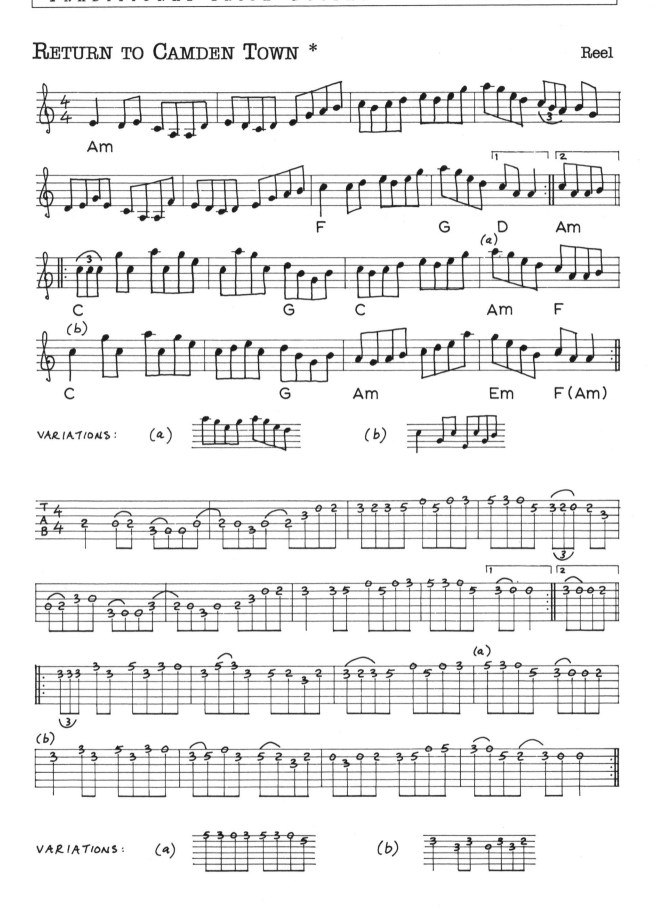

McFADDEN'S HANDSOME DAUGHTER *

Reel

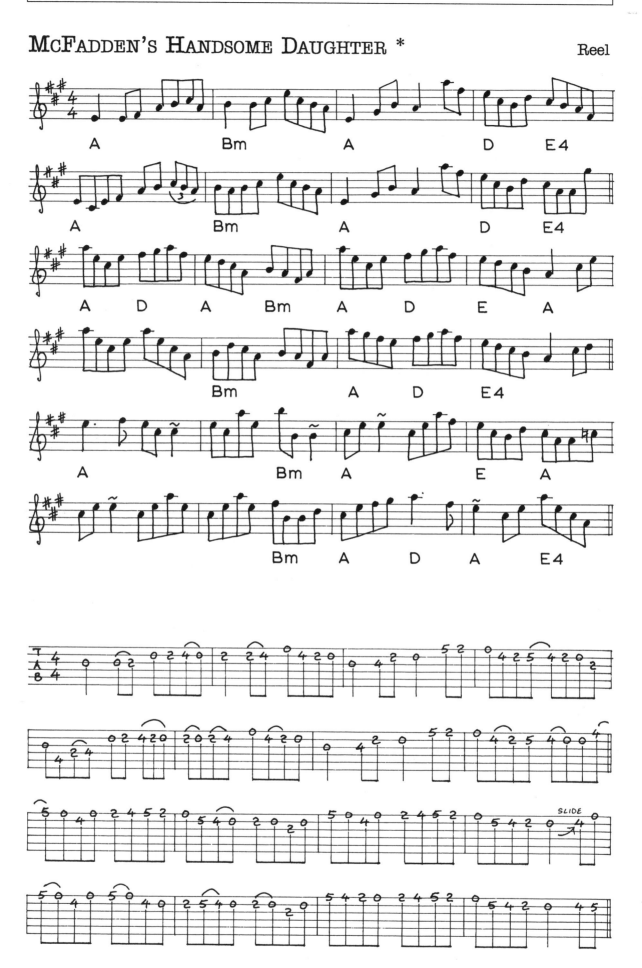

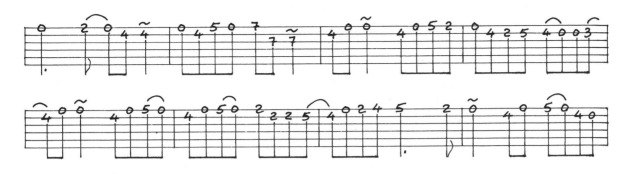

O'Dowd's No. 9 *

Reel

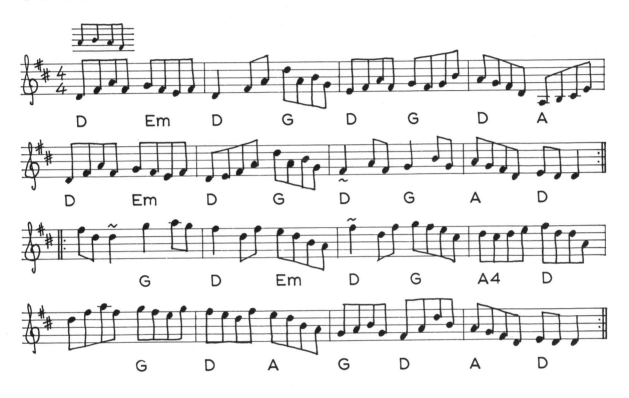

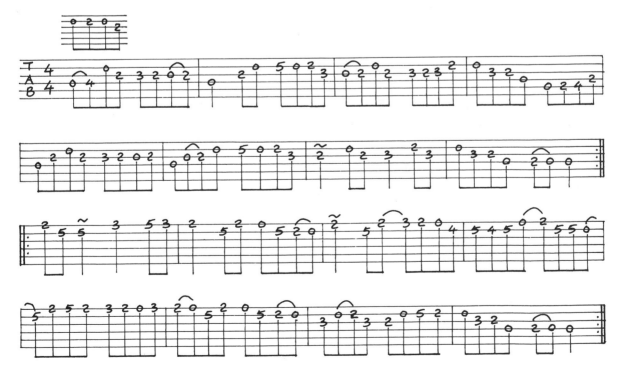

ELVIS PRESLEY'S JIG * (comp. Paul de Grae)

Jig

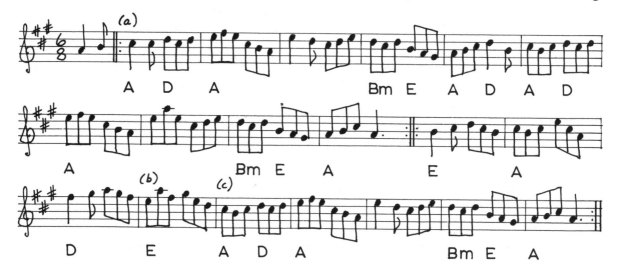

VARIATIONS: (a)   (b)   (c)

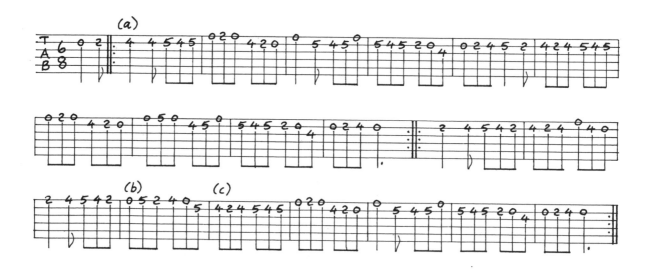

VARIATIONS: (a)   (b)   (c)

THE CORDAL JIG *

Jig

VARIATIONS: (a)   (b)

VARIATIONS: (a)   (b)

TONRA'S JIG *

Jig

VARIATIONS: (a)   (b)   (c)

VARIATIONS: (a)   (b)   (c)

Elvis Presley's is not, of course, a traditional Irish jig. I was taken to see the Elvis movie 'G.I. Blues' at an impressionable age, and I still vividly recall him singing 'Wooden Heart', in German and English, to a little wooden puppet. The idea of rewriting the original German folk tune in Irish style (first as a hornpipe, then as a jig) came to me after hearing Séamus Begley play Carolan's *Fanny Power* followed by Marty Robbins's *El Paso* for an old-time waltz at a ceili.

In the first two tunes, the timing needs close attention: *Elvis Presley's* is in the usual jig time of 6/8, but it has an unusual number of bars in each part, while *The Cordal Jig* just gives that impression - it has the standard eight bars to each part, but has an interesting way of doubling back on itself at the endings. If not going into another tune, finish *The Cordal Jig* with the bar indicated.

The Cordal Jig was so called by Denis Murphy, after the village near Castleisland, County Kerry. It was composed by Walter 'Piper' Jackson, 'the most celebrated Irish piper of the eighteenth century, or perhaps of any age', according to O'Neill in 'Irish Minstrels and Musicians'. The tune appears under the inscrutable title *Jackson's Bouner Bougher* in 'Jackson's Celebrated Irish Tunes', published by Edmund Lee in the late 18th century (my thanks to Dave 'Piper' Hegarty of Fermoy and Tralee for giving me a copy). Unusually for a piping tune, *Jackson's Bouner Bougher* is in the key of C. Also in C is O'Neill's elaborate nine-part setting, called *Morgan Rattler*. I prefer Denis Murphy's two-part version, which also is in a more accessible key, although like some of the most interesting Irish melodies, the key itself is not immediately apparent. For the first few bars it could be E minor or D, until the tune seems to settle on D; but it ends on E, so maybe it's in E minor after all? In fact it's a mix of both, and shows once again that trying to fit traditional tunes into musical pigeon-holes is like nailing jelly to the ceiling.

Tonra's jig is named after its composer who is, according to Breathnach, a musician from County Mayo long resident in America. The repeated notes in the second part are characteristic of the fiddle style of Paddy O'Sullivan (see pages 47 & 63), on whose playing this setting is based.

JIMMY LYON'S HIGHLAND

Highland

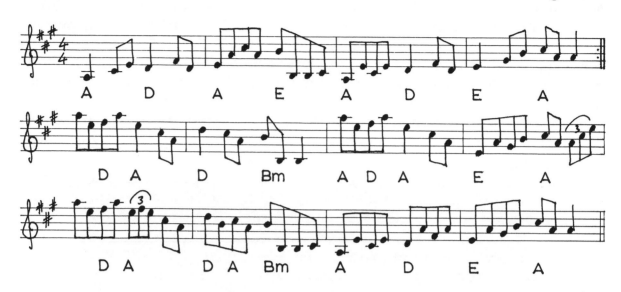

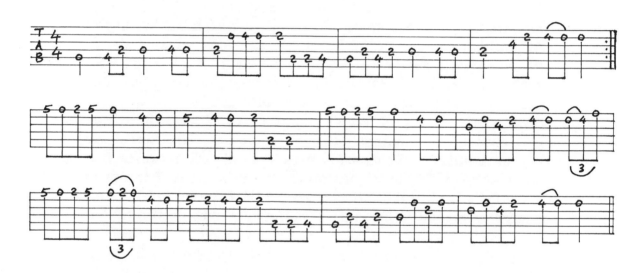

THE TEELIN HIGHLAND

Highland

The traditional music of Donegal is influenced by the cultural connections between that county and Scotland, and Donegal musicians include in their repertoire such Scottish forms as highlands, strathspeys, etc., which until recently were almost unknown in the rest of Ireland. Some of these tunes originated in Scotland but there are also many tunes composed in Donegal using Scottish forms - highlands in particular, because the highland was a very popular dance in Donegal, and there was a demand for tunes to suit.

A highland is played rather like a fast hornpipe; some players end each part with a 'Scotch snap' (a pair of notes in the reverse of the usual dotted rhythm, having the short note first), which gives a more Scottish effect. These two highlands come from the fiddle playing of Mairéad Ní Mhaonaigh, heard in Miltown Malbay some years ago; she has since recorded them with Altan on 'The Red Crow' (Green Linnet 1109). *Jimmy Lyon's* is a version of the Scott Skinner strathspey *Glenlivet* (also called *The Minmore Schottische*).

THE COLLIER'S JIG

Jig

THE COLLIER'S REEL

Reel

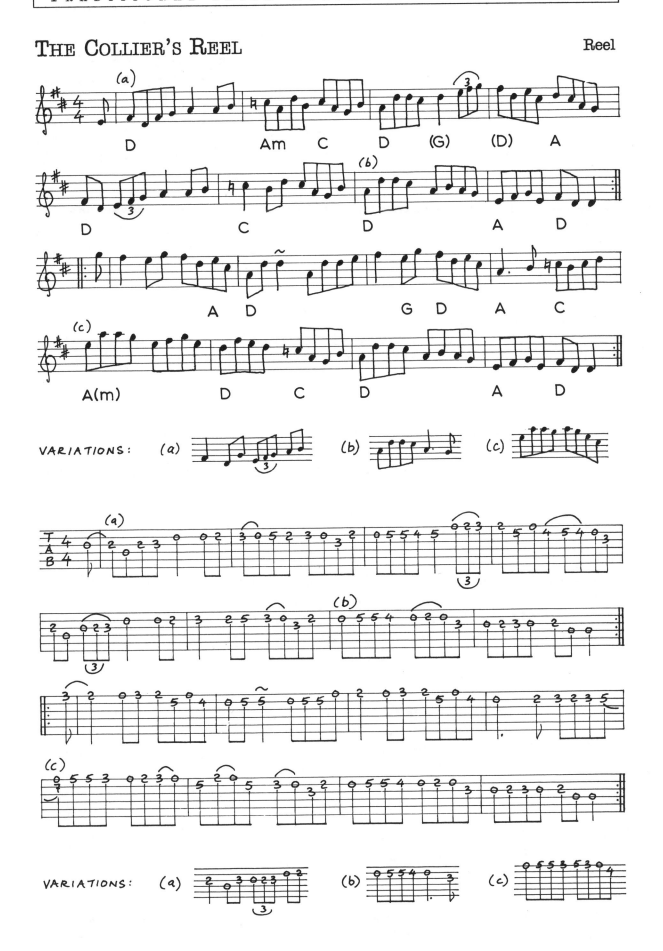

Of the three main forms of Irish dance and dance music - jig, reel and hornpipe - the jig is the oldest, dating back at least as far as the 17th century, although few if any of the surviving jig tunes are as old as that. The reel and the hornpipe seem to have come in around the end of the 18th century, from Scotland and England respectively. We know the origin of many of the reels, and their composers' names, because they were published in contemporary collections in Scotland, but the names of the 18th and 19th century Irish folk composers are, with a very few exceptions, lost to us.

As well as composing new tunes in reel form, Irish musicians clearly adapted existing tunes to suit, and *The Collier's Reel* may have developed from the jig in this way. The jig form appears in the O'Neill collections under the title *Do you want any more?*. Tommy Peoples plays the reel in G (see his book and tape, 'Fifty Irish Fiddle Tunes').

Variation (c) in the jig is a link back to the start of the tune after the repeat of the second part. Try changing some of the C naturals to sharps and vice versa in both these tunes, or even using the occasional F natural instead of F# (see below).

LONESOME NOTES

Sometimes tunes like *The Collier's Jig* are played with a different approach to the 7th note of the scale - C or C# in the key of D, F or F# in the key of G, etc. Seventh and also third notes have an interestingly variable status in Irish melodies, and are sometimes called 'lonesome notes'. The notes C and F are favourites for this sort of treatment, although other notes can also be inflected in this way, depending on the key.

In tunes in G major or A minor, the C note is usually natural, although if used as a passing note or as part of a decoration it may be sharp. In the key of D, both sharp and natural forms are often found in the same tune; in such cases the C may be treated like a 'blue note' in jazz or blues music, being somewhere between B and D, but not necessarily identical with so-called true C or C# as played on a piano ('so-called', because of the compromises of equal temperament - see page 21).

The note F is also something of a chameleon. In A minor it is usually sharp, leading up to or down from G. In G and D major it may be 'true' F# or a sort of indeterminate slide up from E. F natural is not the easiest note to produce on some instruments (I'm not talking about concert pitch here, but F in relation to a nominal D on, say, the open D string of a fiddle or the bottom note of a flute). It may be easier in one octave than another, and it is not unheard of to find both sharp and natural forms in the same tune, which in the key of D effectively means the tune hovers between major and minor - the sort of thing which would give an old-school classical musician an attack of the vapours. The setting of *Garrett Barry's Jig* on the next page is an example.

Players of instruments with fixed notes, such as accordion and concertina, must choose one or other form of these notes, but guitarists have the option of bending the note - admittedly at the risk of putting the string out of tune, but you have to take risks sometimes with your music.

GARRETT BARRY'S JIG *

Jig

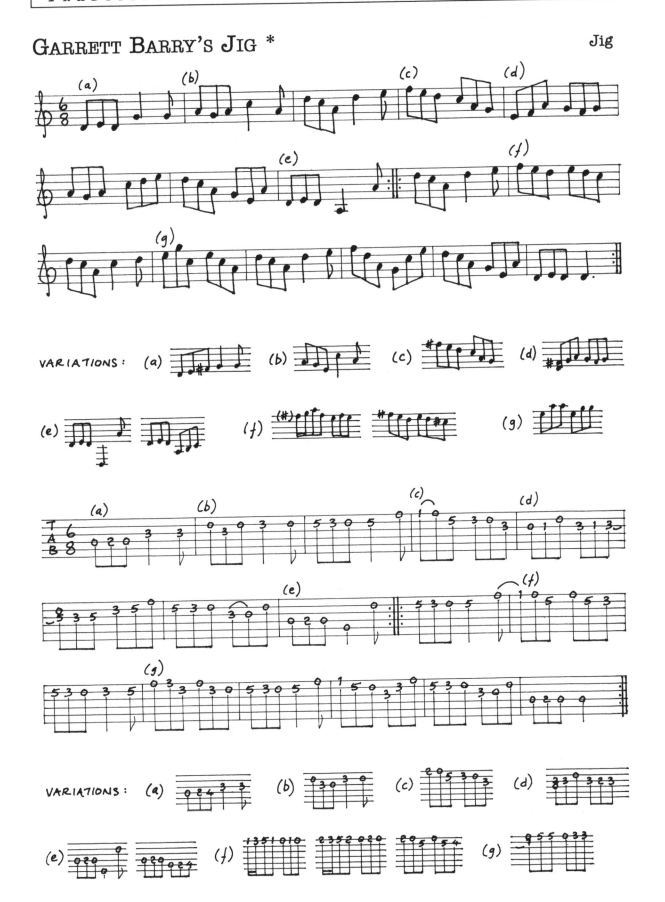

MICK MULCAHY'S JIG *

Jig

VARIATIONS: (a)    (b)

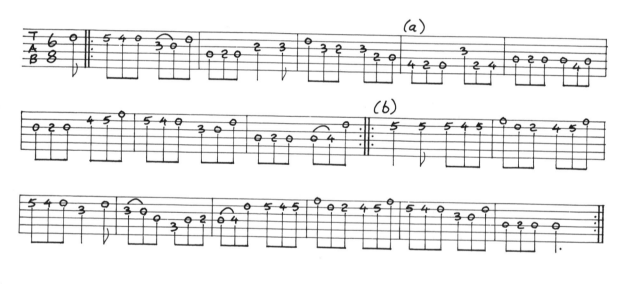

VARIATIONS: (a)    (b)

Breathnach's setting of *Garrett Barry's Jig* is from Willie Clancy, who learned it from his father Gilbert, who in turn learned it from Garrett Barry himself, the famous Clare piper, who died in the Ennistymon workhouse in 1899. Kevin Burke and Jackie Daly recorded a lovely version of *Garrett Barry's* as both a jig and a hornpipe on 'Eavesdropper' (Green Linnet 3002). This tune is a good example of the 'lonesome note' effect described on page 90. Some people play it with F natural throughout, some with F# throughout, but more often the inflection of the F note is a matter of interpretation; likewise some of the C notes. On the recording, *Garrett Barry's* starts in D minor and gradually drifts into D major.

In accompanying such tunes, there are two possible approaches. You can use the sort of major/minor chords shown in Part 2, that is, chords which omit the 'mi' (III) note which defines major and minor. Alternatively, if you know what the melody player is going to do, you can use definite major or minor chords as appropriate to highlight the changes in the tune.

Note the similarity between the end of *Garrett Barry's* and the start of *Mick Mulcahy's*, which I learned from the accordion playing of Mick Mulcahy, a member of the famous Brosna Ceili Band, now living in Abbeyfeale, County Limerick. This tune is also associated with Willie Clancy, and has been recorded by Buttons and Bows as *The Cúl Aodh Jig*. It's commonly played in either G or A, but I liked Mick's version in the lower key of D, and especially his use of the flattened 7th (C natural) in the second part, which caught me by surprise the first time I heard it. It gives that section of the tune a completely different feel to the usual version - try playing a C# to hear the difference.

CHIEF O'NEILL'S VISIT *

Hornpipe.

The title is from O'Neill, and is presumably his own invention; his setting is less flamboyant than this in the second part. O'Neill includes it among the hornpipes, but it's usually played faster, more like a Scottish or Shetland hornpipe, and in even rhythm as opposed to dotted-quaver rhythm. That was how I first heard it played by Máire O'Keeffe (fiddle) and Michelle O'Sullivan (concertina). The Shetland group Curlew recorded it as *The Cambridge*, with nifty guitar backing in the Shetland swing style by Dave Jackson.

I suspect that most music tutor books include at least one tune which even the writer has trouble with, and I freely admit to hitting the odd bum note when trying to play *Chief O'Neill's* Visit at speed - hence the cunning idea of slowing it down to normal Irish hornpipe tempo on the recording.

Francis O'Neill

PAT-JOE'S SLIDE *

Slide

VARIATION : (a)

VARIATION : (a)

FROGMORE LODGE * (comp. Paul S. Cranford)   Slide

KATE MULCAHY'S SLIDE *

Slide

The slide is a type of single jig in 12/8 time. The timing is important, especially for accompaniment - some people accompany slides as if they were hornpipes, and this plodding approach destroys the life of the tune. Slides are often played quite fast, which can make strumming in jig rhythm very hard work, but it's worth it. A good example of how it should be done is Tommy O'Sullivan's guitar backing to the slides played by Matt Cranitch and Donal Murphy on 'Sliabh Notes'.

Slides are mainly associated with the music of Sliabh Luachra, but I found these three outside the rather hazy borders of that magical region, or state of mind, as it's also been called. I learned the first one from Donal Murphy of Abbeyfeale, County Limerick, whose lively accordion playing can be heard on 'Sliabh Notes' and on 'Barking Mad' by Four Men & a Dog. Seamus Creagh plays a similar tune called *Art O'Keeffe's* on his album 'Came the Dawn' (Ossian OSS90).

The second tune was composed by fiddle player, musical savant and publisher Paul Cranford, of Cape Breton, Nova Scotia, and my wife and I are honoured that it was named after the gate lodge of our house (where the recording for this book was made). Slides are not a feature of Cape Breton music, but Paul had the chance to hear the real thing on visits to Ireland and decided to try composing one, very successfully in my opinion. It was recorded by Máire O'Keeffe on her album 'Cóisir/House Party' (Gael-Linn 165). Along with many other of Paul's tunes and tunes by other Cape Breton musicians such as Otis Tomas and Paul MacDonald, *Frogmore Lodge* appears in a book called 'Lighthouse Collection' (Cranford Publications, Cape Breton Island, Nova Scotia, Canada, BOC 1HO). I've taken the liberty of changing the key from G to A.

I learned the third slide, and many other tunes, from the fiddle playing of Kate Mulcahy of Camp, County Kerry, now living in Cork.

PART 5: BOOKS

A great many collections of Irish music are now available. Rather than attempt to list them all, I have merely selected a few that I have found particularly useful.

B&S 1-3   Dave Bulmer & Neil Sharpley: *Music from Ireland*; three volumes; Celtic Music, Lincolnshire, England; 1974-76.

CRÉ I-IV   Breandán Breathnach: *Ceol Rince na hÉireann*; four volumes; An Gúm, Dublin; 1963-97.

DMI   Francis O'Neill: *The Dance Music of Ireland (1001 Gems)*; Chicago 1907, and Waltons, Dublin, 1965.

MOI   Francis O'Neill: *Music of Ireland*; Chicago, 1903.

NF   Allen Feldman and Eamonn O'Doherty: *The Northern Fiddler*; Blackstaff Press, Belfast; 1980.

Other printed settings of some of the tunes in this book are listed below, with their alternative titles.

Far From Home:	DMI 530, MOI 1261.
Old John's Jig:	CRÉ I 22.
The Humours of Tullycrine:	CRÉ I 205 (*Chuir mé feisteas ar mo theachsa*).
The New-mown Meadows:	DMI 619 and MOI 1367 (*The Threepenny Bit*).
Miss Monaghan:	CRÉ III 93, DMI 575, MOI 1312, NF 75 (*Stormy Weather*).
The Bird in the Bush:	CRÉ I 87.
Walsh's Hornpipe:	CRÉ II 312.
The Lowdown Jig:	B&S 2 43 (*McGlinchy's*).
Connie O'Connell's Jig:	CRÉ III 15 (*The Two-and-sixpenny Girl*).
The Silver Spire:	CRÉ I 64.
I'm waiting for you:	CRÉ II 176, DMI 711, MOI 1486.
The Silver Spear:	CRÉ I 141.
The Chancellor:	CRÉ III 226 (*Breen's Hornpipe*), CRÉ III 229 (*The Loughill Hornpipe*), DMI 942 (*The Humours of Ballinlass*).
Hardy Man the Fiddler:	DMI 412, MOI 1117, NF 160 (*untitled*).
Moll Roe:	CRÉ II 93, DMI 441, MOI 1169.
Aggie White's Reel:	CRÉ II 186 (*untitled*), NF 242 (*untitled*).
The Humours of Glandart:	DMI 19, MOI 719 (*East at Glandart*), NF 57 (*Darby Gallagher's Jig*), NF 230.
Munster Buttermilk:	CRÉ I 43 (*The Sports of Multyfarnham*).
Father O'Flynn:	DMI 244 and MOI 1031 (*The Top of Cork Road*).
Laington's Reel:	CRÉ II 258 (*untitled*), CRÉ III 117 (*Dillon Brown*).

Jacky Tar:	MOI 1733 *(The Cuckoo's Nest)*.
The Flowers of Edinburgh:	DMI 920, MOI 1746.
The Moving Cloud:	B&S 2 11, 12.
Return to Camden Town:	B&S 3 41.
McFadden's Handsome Daughter:	DMI 554, MOI 1289.
O'Dowd's No. 9:	CRÉ II 165 *(Summer in Ireland)*.
The Cordal Jig:	CRÉ II 50, DMI 257 and MOI 1046 *(Morgan Rattler)*.
Tonra's Jig:	CRÉ III 20.
The Teelin Highland:	NF 80, 173.
Collier's Jig:	DMI 33 and MOI 741 *(Do You Want Any More?)*.
The Collier's Reel:	DMI 646, MOI 1404.
Garrett Barry's Jig:	CRÉ I 46.
Chief O'Neill's Visit:	MOI 1705.

Some other recommendable books are:

Folk Music and Dances of Ireland by Breandán Breathnach (Ossian, 1996, Cork): the best available short survey of the subject, expertly and entertainingly written, and including thirty songs and tunes.

Last Night's Fun by Ciarán Carson (Jonathan Cape, London, 1996): a philosopher's (and humourist's) view of the world as refracted through the lens of Traditional Irish Music. Essential reading.

Pocket Guide to Irish Traditional Music by Ciarán Carson (Appletree Press, Belfast, 1986): an amazingly detailed and informative little book written by a gifted poet and musician.

The Alternate (sic!) *Tunings Guide for Guitar* by Mark Hanson (Amsco Publications, New York, 1991) examines eight of the most commonly used tunings - standard, drop-D, double drop-D (DADGBD), DADGAD, open D, open G, G6 (DGDGBE) and lute or vihuela tuning (EADF#BE) - and also lists many other tunings and the guitarists who use them.

The Irish DADGAD Guitar Book by Sarah McQuaid (Ossian, 1995): an approach to Irish music using the tuning of choice for many guitarists.

Chord Master by Eamonn O'Connor (Ossian, 1995): a reference book for serious accompanists, tells you all you will ever need to know about finding, constructing and naming chords.

PART 6: RECORDINGS

Happily, there are plenty of good recordings of traditional Irish music now available. The following is a brief selection of albums which feature especially good guitar playing or accompaniment on other instruments. Any glaring omissions can be put down to ignorance on my part (but please write to tell me if you think I've missed anything really special).

Excluding recordings of classically-inspired arrangements - which anyhow don't claim to be traditional, and are usually of song airs, Carolan melodies, and the simpler dance tunes - I know of only four albums devoted to traditional Irish music played on the guitar:

Arty McGlynn: 'McGlynn's Fancy' (Emerald BER 011).

Dick Gaughan: 'Coppers and Brass' (Green Linnet 3062).

Dave Evans, Duck Baker, and Dan Ar Bras: 'Irish Reels, Jigs and Hornpipes for Guitar' (Shanachie 97011).

Frank Simon: 'Slipstream' (Green Island Music GIM 1).

Both Arty McGlynn and Dick Gaughan are outstanding guitarists in their different ways, and a lot can be learned from listening to them (Dick Gaughan, of course, plays Scottish tunes too). The Shanachie album has some fine playing by all three guitarists individually, but the music has been adapted to suit the fingerstyle technique rather than vice versa - nothing at all wrong with that in itself, but it limits your ability to play with traditional musicians. Frank Simon uses something like a bluegrass flatpicking technique on Irish dance tunes, and it works quite well.

Other guitarists who have recorded outstanding versions of Irish tunes amongst their other material include Richard Thompson, Martin Simpson, Davy Graham, Pierre Bensusan, and El McMeen.

Any guitarist with an interest in Irish music should have the album by Arty McGlynn and fiddle virtuoso Nollaig Casey:

Arty McGlynn & Nollaig Casey: 'Lead the Knave' (Round Tower MCG 1).

Their second album, **Causeway** (Tara TA 3035), has a more electric sound, and is perhaps less useful to the acoustic guitarist looking for examples of how to play traditional music, but it's well worth a listen in its own right.

Another essential album is 'The Lonesome Touch' by **Martin Hayes & Denis Cahill** (Green Linnet GLCD 1181). The pairing of Martin Hayes's widely acclaimed fiddle playing with Denis Cahill's fluid and highly expressive guitar playing produces some superb music.

Any history of guitar playing in Ireland must include **Ronnie Drew**. In the early 1960s a new chapter in Irish music opened when Ronnie came back from Spain with his guitar and began playing with the musicians who later formed The Dubliners. Although other musicians such as The Clancy Brothers and Tommy Makem were using guitars for song accompaniment at that time, The Dubliners were the first modern group that I know of to accompany Irish dance tunes on the guitar. Ronnie Drew's guitar playing owed little to the jazz-influenced playing on the early 78s, sounding more like the American folk revival style of Pete Seeger, Woody Guthrie or Burl Ives, and while it may seem unsophisticated by today's standards, it was innovative and highly influential at the time.

Paul Brady is the most influential of more recent guitarists, first with The Johnstons and later with innumerable traditional players in Ireland and America, before he launched his solo career as a singer and songwriter. The first recording I heard of Irish music played on guitar was his duet with **Mick Moloney**, *O'Carolan's Concerto*, on the album 'The Johnstons' (Transatlantic TRA 169), back in 1968; and the first recorded guitar version of an Irish dance tune was, I believe, Paul Brady's playing of *Fred Finn's Reel* on 'Andy Irvine, Paul Brady' (Mulligan LUN 008). Mick Moloney has also recorded extensively, and has done important work in researching Irish traditional music in America.

Mícheál Ó Domhnaill has made two essential recordings with Kevin Burke: **Kevin Burke and Mícheál Ó Domhnaill**: 'Promenade' (Mulligan LUN 028/Green Linnet 3010) and 'Portland' (Green Linnet 1041).

The various Bothy Band albums benefit greatly from his accompaniment, as well as that of **Donal Lunny** (usually on bouzouki or keyboards, but a fine guitarist in his own right) and **Tríona Ní Dhomhnaill** on clavinet. Mícheál and Tríona can also be heard on recordings by the groups Relativity and Nightnoise, and Donal Lunny can be heard, well, almost everywhere (I'm glad to say).

Arty McGlynn has played accompaniment on more albums than you can shake a stick at (if that's your idea of a good time, as Groucho said), and anything with his name on it is worth a listen. My own favourites are the Patrick Street recordings (Green Linnet), and Cathal Hayden's 'Handed Down' (Sharpe Music RBC 116).

Other good role models for guitar accompanists include:

the ever-excellent **Steve Cooney** on his own album with Séamus Begley Begley, 'Meitheal' (Hummingbird 0004), and on many others including Kevin and Seamus Glackin's 'Northern Lights' (Gael Linn 140);

Mark Kelly on the Altan albums (Green Linnet) - **Daithi Sproule** also plays on some of these;

Tommy O'Sullivan on his solo album 'Legacy' (L001) and with Matt Cranitch and Donal Murphy on 'Sliabh Notes' (Cross Border Media CBM 018);

Mick Daly on 'Crossings' by the group Any Old Time (Dara 072) and on 'Barking Mad' by Four Men and a Dog (*Cross Border Media CBM001*);

Gerry O'Beirne on Patrick Street's 'Irish Times' (Green Linnet 1105) and Kevin Burke's 'Up Close' (Green Linnet 1052);

Brendan O'Regan, Kevin Hough and **Chris Kelly** on 'Ceol Tigh Neachtain - Music from Galway'; Chris Kelly also plays with the group Reel Time;

John Doyle on Eileen Ivers's first album (Green Linnet 1139) and her 'Wild Blue' (Green Linnet 1166)

My own contributions to the genre are on Jackie Daly's 'Many's a Wild Night' (Gael Linn 176), Eoin Duignan's 'Coumeenole' (Gael Linn 163) and with Gerry Harrington and Eoghan O'Sullivan 'The Smoky Chimney' (Foetain Spin CD 1001).

If you want to hear how Martin Carthy uses the 'Irish' tuning which he invented, listen to any of his excellent solo albums, or those with Dave Swarbrick, Steeleye Span, The Albion Country Band or Brass Monkey (as mentioned in Part 2, he uses a somewhat different tuning - CGCDGA - on his later recordings).

You can learn a lot from the bouzouki playing of **Alec Finn** on the various De Danann albums, and with Mary Bergin ('Feadóga Stáin': Gael Linn 071) and Frankie Gavin ('Frankie Gavin and Alec Finn': Shanachie 29008). His deceptively simple style conceals a formidable talent and a thorough grasp of the music which make him one of the best accompanists around.

Some other string players who can be listened to for pleasure and instruction are:

Donal Lunny, whose influence on Irish music is incalculable, and who is always worth hearing;

Irish music's best kept secret, **Johnny Moynihan**, who first introduced the bouzouki into Irish music, plays many other instruments as well, and is a great singer - he has recorded with Sweeney's Men, De Danann and Planxty;

Garry Ó Briain, who plays mando-cello and piano with Buttons & Bows and Skylark, and on Jackie Daly's 'Many's a Wild Night';

Andy Irvine, whose bouzouki and mandolin playing is wonderfully melodic and inventive;

Ciaran Curran, bouzouki player with Altan;

and **Cyril O'Donoghue**, bouzouki and guitar, who has recorded with Josephine Marsh and Tola Custy.

Piano accompaniment has come a long way since the days of the 'piano drivers' who pounded away relentlessly on some of the old 78s. **Charlie Lennon** is well known as a fiddle player and composer, and his skill as a soloist surely contributes to his lovely style as a piano accompanist. **Patsy Broderick** plays on Macalla's two albums, and is currently a member of Arcady; as well as being a fine accompanist, she has a great style of melody playing - a rare gift. **Carl Hession** brings an interesting tinge of jazz to his work with Frankie Gavin, and can also be heard as part of the group Moving Cloud and on solo recordings. As for solo piano, the inventiveness and sheer musicality of **Mícheál Ó Súilleabháin** are an inspiration to us all.

Piano technique is not directly adaptable to guitar accompaniment, but the principle of basing the accompaniment on a thorough knowledge of the tune is an important one - perhaps the most important.

From further afield, the piano style of Cape Breton (Nova Scotia) was a revelation to me when Máire O'Keeffe brought back some recordings from there. As in Shetland, accompaniment is an integral part of the fiddle music of Cape Breton, and the piano players are often accomplished fiddlers as well (Howie MacDonald, John Morris Rankin, etc.). The piano style is very lively, with much use of syncopation and walking bass lines - reminiscent of New Orleans piano at times. Guitar is often used in conjunction with piano backing, as on recordings of Winston 'Scotty' Fitzgerald, Jerry Holland, The Rankin Family, and many more. Máire O'Keeffe's own album 'Cóisir/House Party' (Gael Linn 165), recorded in Cape Breton, is a wonderful blend of Irish fiddle music with Cape Breton accompaniment.

Guitarist (and fiddler) **Dave MacIsaac** has recorded a solo album of Cape Breton music played on guitar, 'Celtic Guitar' (Unity Gain Records 1002), and an album with a small band, 'Nimble Fingers' (Picking Productions 02 50399).

Finally, a dazzling example of how a well thought-out backing can bring out unexpected levels of musical expression is 'Hidden Ground' (Tara 2009) by **Paddy Glackin** and **Jolyon Jackson**. This is a good few years old now, but still bears repeated listening. Jackson (whose untimely death was a great loss to music in Ireland) uses a wide range of instruments - mainly keyboards, also guitar, whistle, 'cello, percussion, and quite possibly the kitchen sink - to provide a richly textured setting for Glackin's impressive fiddle playing. The result is hardly 'traditional', but the vigour and depth of feeling of the music not only survive but are enhanced.

Index of Tunes

* Tunes marked with an asterisk are included on the recording.

Ossian Publications

publish and distribute a huge range of Irish and Scottish music,
with items ranging from collections of Irish songs, to tune
collections and instruction books for individual instruments.
We also serve as distributors of the main catalogues of most
Irish Music book publishers and record labels.
For our complete lists of Books, Videos and CDs please contact:

Music Sales Limited
Newmarket Road, Bury St. Edmunds,
Suffolk IP33 3YB
www.musicsales.co.uk

O S S I A N

CONTENTS

1

The New-mown Meadows / Miss Monaghan / The Bird in the Bush (Reels)
melody: Stratocaster, tuning DADEAE accompaniment: acoustic guitar, tuning DADEAE
4:02

2

Elvis Presley's jig (*Paul de Grae*) / The Cordal jig / Tonra's jig
melody & accompaniment: acoustic guitar, tuning DADEAE, capo III
3:12

3

The Humours of Tullycrine (slow air)
Stratocaster solo, tuning DADEAE
2:13

4

The Humours of Tullycrine (hornpipe)
melody & accompaniment: acoustic guitar, tuning DADEAE
2:13

5

Father O'Flynn / The Bees in the Heather / Paddy O'Sullivan's jig
melody & accompaniment: acoustic guitar, tuning DADEAE
4:25

6

The Drunken Landlady / Up the Track (*Joe Thoma*)
melody: acoustic, tuning EADEAE, capo II, accompaniment: ditto, but DADEAE
3:02

7

Jackie Tar *solo acoustic guitar, tuning EADEAE* / The Flowers of Edinburgh, (hornpipes)
melody & accompaniment: acoustic guitar, tuning EADEAE
3:24

8

Hardy man the Fiddler / Moll Roe,
melody & accompaniment: acoustic guitar, tuning DADEAE
2:32

9

The Moving Cloud (*Neilie Boyle*) / Aggie White's reel (*Paddy Kelly*)
intro. & melody: Stratocaster, tuning DADGBE (drop-D) double-tracked in octaves on second tune.
accompaniment: acoustic guitar, tuning DADEAE, capo V
4:20

10

Old John's jig
melody & accompaniment: acoustic guitar, tuning DADEAE
3:12

11

Walsh's hornpipe / Chief O'Neill's visit
melody & accompaniment: acoustic guitar, tuning DADEAE
3:12

12

Garrett Barry's jig / Mick Mulcahy's jig
solo acoustic guitar, tuning DADEAE
3:49

13

Return to Camden Town / McFadden's Handsome Daughter / O'Dowd's no.9 (Reels)
melody: Stratocaster, tuning DADEAE accompaniment: acoustic guitar, tuning DADEAE, capo V, VII and V.
4:08

14

Pat-Joe's Slide / Frogmore Lodge (*Paul S.Cranford*) / Kate Mulcahy's Slide
melody & acccompaniment: acoustic guitar, tuning DADEAE
2:42

15

Sonny Riordan's polka / The last of June
melody: Stratocaster, tuning DADEAE, accompaniment: acoustic guitar, tuning DADEAE
3:19